DON'T STOP...

Canter into your

PONY ANNUAL
2021

This annual belongs to

Sarah O.

INSIDE

The lowdown on leading, p72

Create an awesome work of art, p12

Published by DJ Murphy (Publishers) Ltd, Marlborough House, Headley Road, Grayshott, Surrey GU26 6LG

Who did what in PONY – The Annual
Contributors Jo Browne, Kiera Boyle, Megan Hurley, Bethany Searby
Design Adam Witt, Jake Booth

PONY magazine is published every four weeks. To find out more about PONY magazine, visit ponymag.com
© Copyright DJ Murphy (Publishers) Ltd 2020

Printed by Graphicom via dell'Industria – 36100 Vicenza, Italy

ISBN 978-0-9928279-9-1

6 **A-Z OF PONIES**
Awesome facts about your fave animal

10 **ALL ABOUT EVENTING**
An epic guide to this super-fun sport

12 **MAKE A PONY PAINTING**
It's time to get creative

14 **THE GREAT OUTDOORS**
Why hacking's so amazing

18 **SHRUNK IN THE WASH**
Pebbles gets a big shock after a bath

20 **BE AN EVENTING STAR**
A fun board game to play with friends

22 **EVENTS: ROYAL WINDSOR**
Take a trip to the famous horse show

24 **COMMON SENSE**
Find out about your pony's senses

26 **SIBLING RIVALRY**
A fun photo story about two sisters

30 **WORLD BREEDS: CASPIAN HORSE**
A breed with an incredible history

32 **POLE-ISH YOUR PONY'S PACES**
Amazing polework exercises to try

36 **THE SAND PONY**
Art comes to life in this cool story

38 **HOW MUCH DO YOU LOVE PONIES?**
Will you ace our test?

40 **KEEP YOUR PONY HAPPY**
How to meet all of his needs

44 QUIZ **GET SET AND VET**
Test your pony health knowledge

YOUR ANNUAL...

Awesome jumping exercises, p54

46 FOALIN' AROUND
Facts about super-cute foals

48 PLAIT'S AMAZING!
A step-by-step guide to plaiting your fave pony's mane and tail

52 PONY PUZZLES
Fun and games to entertain you

54 JUMP FOR FUN
Ideas for an awesome jumping sesh

58 ALL THE COLOURS
Pony colours and markings

60 THE SECRET YARD
A dream comes true for Lydia when she discovers some empty stables

62 EVENTS: CHATSWORTH INTERNATIONAL HORSE TRIALS
A super-popular three-day event

64 WORLD BREEDS: MUSTANG
The wild horse with a huge personality

66 GET THE PARTY STARTED
Invite friends to an awesome sleepover

68 ALL SQUARE
How to halt like a top dressage rider

70 QUIZ CARE PACKAGE
A quiz about looking after ponies

72 LEAD THE WAY
Be a pro at handling ponies

76 FUN WITH FLAGS
A photo story about mounted games

80 FESS UPS
Confessions of riding school ponies

82 WORLD BREEDS: MARWARI
A horse with the most amazing ears

84 QUIZ PONY CAREER PATHS
Discover your dream horsey job

86 EVENTS: GLOBAL CHAMPIONS TOUR
An awesome showjumping series

88 HORSESCOPES
What's in store for you in 2021

92 CUTE AS A BUTTON
How adorable is your fave pony?

94 WORLD BREEDS: PRZEWALSKI'S HORSE
Learn about a unique breed

96 DON'T TRY THIS AT HOME
Adrenalin-fuelled horse sports

98 TO THE RESCUE
A story about an eventful hack

100 ANSWERS AND TEMPLATES
Quiz solutions and make templates

102 CHARLIE'S BACK...
...and he's causing mayhem

THE A-Z OF PONIES

Awesome info about your fave animal!

There's so much to know and learn about ponies, and our brilliant A-Z is the perfect place to start! Read on to discover 26 epic facts about your fave animal.

B is for bombproof

This word describes a pony who's super-chilled and isn't scared by anything – even loud noises or flapping plastic! You might see it mentioned in ponies for sale ads. Don't worry if this doesn't sound like your pony – you can spend time in the arena spook-proofing him so he takes everything in his stride. Put out some obstacles like cones, signs and dustbins that you might see on a hack, then gradually introduce him to them.

E is for equine

Equine is a general term for horses and ponies, and it can refer to donkeys as well! You may hear it mentioned in lots of different parts of the horseworld – for example, an equine vet specialises in horses, and equine college is where you can go to learn even more about your fave animal!

F is for feathers

It's not just chickens that have feathers! It's also the name for the hair that grows around a pony's lower legs. Some horses have more feather than others – heavier breeds have loads which drapes down over their hooves, but fine ponies only have a little.

I is for instructor

If you love ponies, this is one of the most important people you'll know! Having regular lessons with a qualified instructor will help you grow and improve as a rider, and they'll teach you how to get the best out of every pony you ride. They'll know clever ways to boost your confidence, and they will let you in on loads of awesome schooling exercises to try, too!

J is for jumping

Soaring over fences on your fave pony is epic! It'll give you an incredible feeling when they power over a fence and clear it with ease! All you'll need to do is work out which is your absolute fave – showjumping over coloured fences, or galloping through the countryside to tackle a cross-country course of natural obstacles.

A is for aids

Your aids are super-important because you use them to communicate with your fave pony when you're riding him! The term refers to your hands, legs, voice, weight and seat when you use them to give subtle instructions to your pony that let him know what you want him to do. You'll use your aids to ask him to walk on and halt, and to perform school movements from simple circles to more advanced exercises such as leg-yield and turn-on-the-forehand.

DID YOU KNOW?

Your whip's known as an artificial aid.

C is for chestnut

Chestnut is a beautiful golden coat colour, but it's also something you'll find on your pony's legs! If you carefully run your hand down the inside of his foreleg, you'll feel a hard lump just above his knee – this is a chestnut. There's usually one on each leg, and they're just under the hock on the hind limbs. Some people think they're the remains of an extra toe ponies had millions of years ago – wow!

D is for dressage

If you and your pony love flatwork, why not show off your moves by entering a dressage test? It's something anyone can try, as some tests only require you to walk and trot! You never know, you might be bitten by the bug, and decide to move up the levels and see how far you can go. You could even be the next Carl Hester or Charlotte Dujardin!

G is for gallop

Your fave pony's fastest pace is amazing to experience – you'll feel like you're flying! The best place to try it out is on a gallops, which is a long stretch of track that's specially designed for horses and ponies to really open up their stride! There may be one in your area that you can hire out.

DID YOU KNOW?

When your pony's galloping there'll be a moment of suspension when all four of his feet are off the ground!

H is for hooves

Your pony's hooves support his weight and enable him to move around, so it's really important to keep them in good condition. They also help his blood to circulate, too! Every time he takes a step, the frog on the underside of his hoof acts as a pump to send blood up his leg and around his body. You can help keep your fave pony's feet healthy by picking them out once a day, giving him a healthy diet and making sure he sees the farrier regularly.

K is for keepers

A small but important part of your fave pony's bridle, keepers are leather loops that you tuck all the straps into. They make sure your pony looks smart, with no flapping bits of leather, and help prevent the buckles coming undone, too. Before you mount for your ride, do a quick check to ensure all those straps are neatly tucked in.

L is for lungeing

This is a way to exercise your fave pony from the ground, and involves him working in a circle around you. It's useful if you don't have time to ride, and is used a lot to teach young horses how to respond to voice aids and accept a rein contact. Only experienced people should lunge, though, so if you think your fave pony would benefit, ask your instructor to do it for you.

DID YOU KNOW?

You can have a riding lesson on the lunge, too! It's a great way to improve, as your instructor controls your pony while you just focus on your position.

O is for open order

When you have a group lesson and everyone goes one behind the other, it's called riding in closed order. Open order is when you get to freestyle it, and ride independently of everyone else! It'll test your control and ability to give the pony you're riding clear instructions, but you still need to obey the rules of the school. So, find your own space, keep your distance from the other ponies and, if you find you're riding towards someone, remember to pass them left side to left side.

P is for PONY mag

Want to find out even more awesome facts about ponies and riding – then look no further than *PONY mag*! Every issue's packed full of great ways to have loads of fun, and you can even get your own fave pony featured if you send in a photo!

T is tack

This is pretty vital if you want to enjoy a ride on your fave pony! Tack's a general term that means his saddle and bridle, but it also refers to any piece of kit you use for him, from his girth and saddlepad to his boots and neckstrap.

U is for unsound

Unfortunately, ponies sometimes go lame, which is also known as being unsound. If you think your pony's lame, tell your yard manager straightaway and call your vet out to take a look. They'll probably ask you to trot your pony up, so they can work out which leg's hurting him.

W is for withers

This is a bony ridge at the end of your fave pony's neck, just in front of where his saddle sits. It's the point he's measured from to find out how high he is!

DID YOU KNOW?

Ponies are measured in hands, and one hand equals 4in or 10.16cm. So, a pony who's 14.2hh is 148cm high!

X is for X-ray

If you're worried your pony's hurting somewhere, you can ask your vet to do an X-ray. It's useful for finding out what's going on in his legs and hooves, and can diagnose tooth probs, too.

M is for mounting

Before you can enjoy a ride on your fave pony, you'll need to get into the saddle! Always take care to mount safely, and do it in a way that's comfy for your pony. Use a mounting block to avoid pulling the saddle over to one side, and take care to land lightly on his back. If he's a bit fidgety, ask someone experienced to stand at his head for you.

N is for native breed

These are breeds of horse and pony who originate from the UK or Ireland, such as Shetlands, Welsh ponies, New Forests, Dartmoors, Fells, Exmoors and Connemaras. Native breeds make awesome all-round riding ponies for children. They're super-popular because they'll turn a hoof to any activity, and they're hardy types who are easy to care for.

Q is for quarters

The rear part of your pony is known as his quarters – or hindquarters to be more accurate! It's a strong, well muscled area that powers him along when he moves, and pushes him up and over fences when you're jumping.

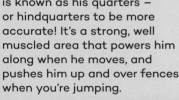

R is for rolling

Ponies love to roll, and the muddier the patch the better! It helps them scratch their itchy spots, and it's a great way to remove loose hair when their coat's changing. Your fave pony's sure to enjoy a roll after he's been ridden – and definitely after you've given him a bath!

S is for schoolmaster

If you're learning to ride, you need one of these! It's a pony who's been there, done it and got the t-shirt, and will show you the ropes. You can also get schoolmasters who are awesome at dressage and jumping, and who help more experienced riders refine their skills.

V is for veteran

Once a pony reaches his 15th birthday, he's officially known as a veteran! However, this is actually quite young for a pony, and many stay active into their 20s and beyond! If you have an older pony, it's important to take extra care of him to help make sure he stays fit and healthy.

Y is for yearling

When a young pony reaches his first birthday, he's known as a yearling. At this age, ponies are super-inquisitive and have a lot of growing to do! They're way too young to be ridden, so spend lots of time hanging out in the field with their friends. It's a good time to get them used to being handled, though, so they take everything in their stride as they grow up.

Z is for Zorse

We're not making it up – honest! A zorse is a cross between a zebra and a horse, where the dad's stripy and the mum's a mare. If it's the other way round, and the mum's a zebra, the foal's called a hebra! Other zebroid hybrids include a zonkey (half donkey) and zebrula (half mule).

All about EVENTING

Find out why eventing's the most exciting sport to try with your fave pony

E venting's the ultimate equestrian sport to have a go at because it tests your skills in three different disciplines – dressage, showjumping and cross-country. To be in with a chance of acing all three phases you'll need to have an awesome partnership with your fave pony.

Dress to impress

For the dressage and showjumping, you'll need to wear breeches or jods, a competition shirt, show jacket, riding hat and riding boots. You'll get a chance to stand out from the crowd in the cross-country phase, though, as you can wear a colourful top and hat silk! For XC you also need a skull cap and a body protector. Both of these must meet the latest safety standards.

DID YOU KNOW?

During the winter, you can have a go at arena eventing competitions. They involve jumping a course of showjumps and cross-country style fences, all in an arena!

The phases

1 DRESSAGE

You'll be asked to show how balanced, supple and responsive your pony is by performing a series of movements in walk, trot and canter. The dressage phase always comes first.

2 SHOWJUMPING

The challenge is to go clear around a course of 8-12 coloured fences, and be within the time allowed. It's the second phase at a one-day event, but comes at the end of a three-day event. It's an exciting climax to a three-day comp as the riders go in reverse order, with the highest placed competitors jumping last.

3 CROSS-COUNTRY

This is what every competitor's been waiting for – the chance to gallop around a course of natural fences! There's usually 16-25 obstacles, which could include steps, a corner, water and ditches. You'll be timed, too, so your aim is to finish clear and as close as possible to the optimum time.

How it's scored

To be in with a chance of a rosette, you'll need to complete all three phases with the lowest number of penalties. This means performing an amazing dressage test, then going clear in both the showjumping and cross-country, without picking up any time penalties!

DID YOU KNOW?

Eventing competitions usually take place over one or three days.

Watch it

If you want to see eventing at its very best, head to Badminton or Burghley Horse Trials. They're two of the most famous events in the world, and are ones every top rider dreams of winning!

Roll of honour

Discovered your new fave sport? Why not aspire to be like these riding heroes...

← Piggy March
Aced the famous Badminton Horse Trials in 2019.

Pippa Funnell →
One of only two winners of the super-challenging Rolex Grand Slam, which involves winning three major events back to back.

← Michael Jung
Olympic champion in 2012 and 2016, and the only other Rolex Grand Slam winner.

William Fox-Pitt →
Has won Burghley Horse Trials a record six times!

A PONY PRINT
CANVAS

Make a gorgeous piece of art to hang up on your bedroom wall

TOP TIP
A pony canvas would make a great present for a friend or horsey relative!

YOU'LL NEED

✓ a canvas
✓ two foam sheets
✓ glue
✓ scissors
✓ two sheets of card
✓ paint
✓ a pen
✓ a paintbrush

1. Paint the canvas your fave colour and let it dry.

Turn to p101 for the templates

Ask an adult for help when using scissors.

2. Make your stamps by tracing around the horse head and horseshoe templates, then cut them out with scissors.

3. Place your templates on top of the foam sheets and draw around them. You'll need three of each design. Then cut them out.

4. Fold each piece of card in half, then in half again. Glue the sides of each folded sheet together.

TOP TIP
You could also use thicker card or cardboard for the base of your stamp.

5. Stack your foam horse head shapes on top of each other and glue them together. Do the same with the horseshoes, then stick each design onto a piece of folded card.

6. Brush a thin layer of paint onto the bottom of the horse head stamp. It's a good idea to test out your first stamp on a spare sheet of paper to make sure it'll look how you'd like it.

7. Repaint your stamp, and press it down onto the canvas. Make sure it's the right way up and press it as evenly as you can.

8. Now create your own pattern using the horse head and horseshoe stamps! You could even use more than one colour.

TOP TIP
Add some glitter glue to the horseshoes for a bit of extra sparkle.

WOW!

When you're finished, let your canvas dry. Then hang it up somewhere you'll see it everyday!

THE GREAT OUTDOORS

Why riding out's the most amazing thing you can do with your fave pony

Going for a hack isn't just great exercise for your fave pony, he'll love getting out and about and seeing lots of different scenery. It's super-fun for you, too, as you can explore new paths and tracks. Plus, spending time with him this way will make the bond between you even stronger!

See the world outside

There are so many reasons why hacking out's good for your fave pony. It'll keep him interested in his work, as spending too much time in the arena could get a bit boring for him. It'll help him learn to cope with being ridden over different terrain, which is especially useful if you want to compete in cross-country, and he'll see lots of sights and sounds that'll teach him to take anything and everything in his stride!

Where to ride

While you can ride on the roads, it's much better to stay away from the traffic. However, you should only venture onto tracks and open spaces where ponies are allowed, such as...

- **bridleways** – this network of paths is designed for horses and ponies, although walkers and cyclists can use them, too. They're either marked by a blue arrow or a wooden signpost with the word bridleway on it
- **restricted byways** – these are tracks that can be used for riding, as well as for walking and cycling
- **byways open to all traffic** – BOATs are similar to byways, but motor vehicles and motorbikes are allowed on them
- **common land** – ponies are welcome on some open spaces, but before you ride it's important to check whether you can go anywhere or if you need to stick to certain tracks
- **beaches** – a long stretch of golden sand's perfect for a hack, but going to a beach will require a bit of planning. You'll need to find one that's horse friendly and work out when you're allowed to ride there, and what time the tide will be out

BE SAFE, BE SEEN

Whether you're riding on a road or a bridleway, it's super-important that you and your pony wear lots of hi-vis. On the roads, it'll help motorists see you sooner, so they can slow down before they drive past you. On paths and tracks, it'll make you more visible to cyclists, dog walkers and even pilots of low-flying aircraft, so they can avoid you. There's loads of different types of hi-vis available, such as tabards, hat covers and gloves for you, and leg bands, tail guards and ear covers for your pony!

DID YOU KNOW?

Wearing hi-vis gear means a motorist can see you up to three seconds sooner!

The best ride

Some ponies may find hacking very exciting! You can help keep your pony calm by riding out with a friend on a sensible pony, and stick to walk at first. It's really important that you can control your pony in an open space, so practise this in the arena first. Ride lots of transitions from one pace to another to get his attention, and make sure he'll halt obediently when you ask him to.

Something else you can do in the arena is introduce your fave pony to objects you might see on a hack that he could find spooky. So, place bins, cones, road signs and safely secured plastic bags around the arena and introduce him to them gradually. He'll soon realise that they're nothing to worry about, and he'll be less likely to spook when you're out and about.

Fit for action

Hacking's really useful for helping keep your fave pony fit, so he can easily cope with all the activities you want to do with him, such as jumping and schooling! Always build his fitness slowly, though, starting with short hacks in walk before introducing some hillwork and gentle trotting.

TOP TIP
If you usually have lessons at a riding school, why not ask if you can swap a session in the school for a ride out instead?

TOP TIP
Never hack out alone and always tell someone what route you'll be taking and when you expect to get back.

TOP TIP
You can make a hack even more of an adventure by turning it into a picnic ride or a treasure hunt!

Having a blast

Stepping up the pace to canter can be the most exciting thing about riding out, but make sure you've checked the ground's suitable before you go for a blast. It can be best to canter uphill, to help you bring your pony back to a steady trot, then walk. Also, always be courteous to any other people who are using the same tracks, and don't canter if walkers or cyclists are ahead.

A FUN RIDE

Are you keen to explore somewhere new? Then going on a sponsored or fun ride will give you the chance to ride across land that's not usually open to horses. They're epic to go on with friends, and many include jumps you can pop over if you want to. There's usually loads of fun rides through spring, summer and autumn, so ask riders on your yard if they can recommend a good one.

DID YOU KNOW?

Every year a fun ride takes place at Burghley Horse Trials! You can ride through the stunning parkland and see the famous XC jumps up close!

Going the distance

If you and your pony love hacking more than anything else, you can even do it competitively! Endurance is a popular discipline that's just like going on a long hack, but you'll need to complete the route in a certain time, and a vet will check your pony is sound and healthy when he crosses the finish line. Another sport where hacking plays a big part is TREC. This fun sport has three phases and combines riding out in the countryside with doing an obstacle course and showing that you have control over your pony's paces!

Help to stay safe

If you're planning to hack out your fave pony, it's a really good idea to study for and take the British Horse Society's Ride Safe Award. It'll make sure you know all the rules of hacking out, which will help you enjoy the experience even more. If you're a Pony Club member, you can prep for riding on the roads by taking the Mini Road Rider and Road Rider badges.

School's out

You can even polish up your pony's flatwork when you're hacking out! There's loads of different ways to work on improving his paces outside the arena, and you may even find he prefers learning this way. Here are a few ideas to try...

- work on his transitions by asking for a change of pace every few strides, such as going from walk to trot, then trot to walk. You can count out the strides, or make a transition every time you pass a tree or fence post
- ride shallow loops along tracks that are at least 5m wide, to help improve his suppleness and bend
- introduce leg-yield by asking him to take sideways steps from one side of a track to the other
- make his paces adjustable by encouraging him to take longer, then shorter steps in walk and trot

In fact, there's so much you can do out on a hack that you might choose to do more of your schooling in the outdoors!

TOP TIP

Before exploring a new bridleway, ask an adult to walk it with you on foot first. You can check the ground's suitable, and make sure there's nothing spooky on the route that could worry your pony.

SHRUNK IN THE WASH

Who knew one bath could make such a difference to Pebbles!

Pebbles was grazing in his paddock, as he did every morning. The sun had just risen and his best friends, Snickers and Dougal, were munching grass beside him. "Guys," said Snickers, suddenly lifting his head and looking around suspiciously. "Why are the kids here so early?" Pebbles stopped eating and pricked his ears to listen, too. Sure enough, he could hear a babble of excited voices and footsteps nearing the yard. "The school holidays start today," mumbled Dougal, not bothering to look up. Snickers and Pebbles stared at each other in total dismay.

The holidays begin

"Pebbles, Pebbles!" called his owner, Ruby, as she bounded up to him. Pebbles looked up and gratefully accepted the treat Ruby offered him. As he was being led towards the gate, he looked back over his shoulder and saw Snickers trotting away from his owner, Olivia, every time she got close. He was whickering with laughter. "You're so silly," Pebbles called to him. "She loves it really!" Snickers whinnied back in reply.

Eventually, Lindsey, the yard manager, was able to cleverly coax Snickers in with a few pony nuts, so all three stood tied up outside their stables. Snickers and Dougal were being taken out on a hack together by their riders, but Pebbles heard Ruby decide she'd rather go in the school. "Just my luck," he thought.

"Act really naughty so you get to finish early," said Snickers. "He's not like you, Snickers!" Dougal chimed in, snorting with disapproval.

Bath time

The others left the yard and Ruby took Pebbles in the school. Lindsey poked her head over the fence to check they were alright every now and then, but the session went well, and Pebbles found he actually quite enjoyed himself. Ruby dismounted and Pebbles was tied back up and untacked. Lindsey walked over and told her: "I'm just going to pop into the house for breakfast, Ruby. Give me a shout if you need anything."

When Lindsey left, it was just Ruby and Pebbles on the yard. "You're a bit sweaty, Pebbles," Ruby said. "Let's give you a bath." Pebbles groaned. He wasn't a big fan of getting wet. Reluctantly, he allowed himself to be led over to the wash bay and stood patiently while Ruby sprayed him with water, which was a bit cold. "Now, I've got some special new shampoo to try," Ruby explained, showing it to Pebbles. The bottle had a picture of a Falabella pony on the front. Ruby began lathering Pebbles in it, and he wrinkled his nose as it smelled a bit funny and made his skin start to tingle.

All of a sudden, something unbelievable happened. Before Pebbles knew what was going on, a swirl of bubbles whooshed around him. He felt dizzy, and his line of vision seemed to be getting closer and closer to the ground like he was falling over. When the bubbles subsided, Pebbles saw Ruby standing in front of him, but he had to look up as she seemed really tall now. He could see her staring at him in horror.

A new body

Ruby crouched down next to Pebbles in panic and looked him over. "Oh my gosh… you're tiny!" she exclaimed. "What on earth's in that shampoo?" She ran over and started to read the label on the back of the bottle. Pebbles looked down at his now short, stubby legs. "Arghhh!" he whinnied. "Why am I so round and fluffy?" Ruby turned and stared at him again, dropping the shampoo bottle and letting it leak all over the floor. "Now it's gone everywhere!" Pebbles yelled, but all Ruby could hear was a high-pitched neigh. "Oh Pebbles, what've I done to you?" she said, bending down and burying her head into his now tiny neck. "I've turned my beautiful 14hh pony into a Falabella!" Pebbles found he felt sorry for his rider, as he noticed a tear trickle onto his fur. To comfort her, he reached his head round and encased her in a hug.

Looking for answers

Pebbles pricked his tiny ears when he heard a clatter of hooves nearing the gate to the yard. He dreaded what the others would say when they saw him. Snickers would have a field day making fun of his bushy mane and high pitched whinny. "I'll ask the others what to do, Pebbles!" said Ruby, grabbing his leadrope and taking him across the yard with her. Pebbles struggled to keep up with his little legs, so he had to trot quickly behind her. He really didn't like being so small – it was humiliating!

The other ponies and their riders looked at Pebbles questioningly as they walked onto the yard. "Oh my word… who's that?" asked Olivia. "He's so cute!" Snickers and Dougal looked down at Pebbles and sniffed like they were meeting a new pony for the first time. "It's me, Pebbles!" he insisted. Snickers and

Dougal burst out laughing. "Pebbles? Haha, you look ridiculous!" said Snickers.

"What happened?" Dougal asked. Pebbles sighed with frustration. "Ruby must've washed me with some kind of shrinking shampoo!"

"Are you going to stay like that forever?" asked Snickers, trying to stifle his laughter.

"I'd better not!" replied Pebbles, crossly.

"How are we going to get Pebbles back to normal?" Ruby asked her friends, but no one had an answer.

Growing back

Just then, Lindsey strode over from the house. She instantly raised her eyebrows at Pebbles. He still had some soap on him and he found it now felt sticky in his shaggy fur.

"Ruby, is that… Pebbles?" she asked. Everyone nodded in reply and Ruby explained what had happened. Lindsey smiled. "Come on, I know just the thing to turn him back." She took hold of Pebbles and led him back over to the wash bay, while the other ponies were tied up to be untacked. Pebbles stood stock still as Lindsey commanded Ruby to rinse the remaining shampoo off him.

Once he was completely showered and dried off with towels, Pebbles saw Lindsey come out of the tack room holding a tub with a picture of a Shire horse on the front. She carefully scattered some of the purple powder along Pebbles' back, with a rubber glove on. "Growing powder," she explained. The others gathered to watch as, in a cloud of smoke, Pebbles grew taller and taller until he became himself again. They all walked over and hugged him, and Pebbles let out a big sigh of relief. "I'm so sorry, Pebbles," Ruby said, squeezing him tight. "Although… could you put on a little more and make him 14.2hh, Lindsey?" she asked cheekily. Lindsey laughed. "I think that's enough growing and shrinking for one day!" Lindsey bent down and picked up the shrinking shampoo bottle. It still had a bit left inside, even after Ruby had spilled most of it onto the floor. "And I think I'll take this for safe keeping," she added.

Once everyone had gone back to their own ponies, Ruby whispered to Pebbles, "I was only joking. You're the perfect size just as you are."

> All of a sudden something unbelievable happened

BE AN EVENTING STAR

Can you ace our three-day-event game and be crowned the winning rider?

CROSS-COUNTRY

You rode a flawless test! Trot straight to square 12 and get ready to start your cross-country round.

B
4 **5** **6** **7** **8** **9** **10** **11**
F
E
3
K

Oops! You took a wrong turn in your test! Go back three squares.

M
2 **H**

Wow! What a straight centre line! Move forward two squares.

24 **23** **22** **21**
25

Refuse the ditch and go back two squares to try again!

1

DRESSAGE

26

START

27

You're galloping towards the finish line! Move forward two squares.

28
29 **30** **31**

You aced that hedge! Choose a player to skip their next turn.

WHAT YOU NEED

- a dice
- friends to play with
- a counter per player

HOW TO PLAY

Place your counters in the start box and take it in turns to roll the dice (youngest player goes first). Be sure to follow the instructions on the squares you land on! The first player to reach the finish line is the champion!

12 13 14 15 16 17 18 19 20

Your pony did a spectacular jump over that log. Move forward two squares!

Splash! You've fallen in the water! Go back to square 12 and restart your cross-country round.

A pole falls for four penalties! Go back two squares.

FINISH

50 49 48 47 46 45 44 43 42 41 40 39 38 37

Your pony did an amazing jump! Pick a player to miss a turn!

SHOWJUMPING

36 35 34 33 32

Woohoo! You've cleared the first few showjumps! Move forward two squares.

Uh oh, your pony's failed the second trot up. Miss a turn!

WINDSOR HORSE SHOW

This amazing event is held in the grounds of Windsor Castle!

TOP TIP
For the very best views of the action and fast-track entry, join The Royal Windsor Horse Show Club!

Not only is Windsor one of the biggest outdoor horse shows in the UK, it takes place in a world-famous location and you may even spot a member of the royal family!

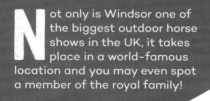

Equestrian extravaganza

Windsor Horse Show has something for everyone and pretty much every equestrian discipline you can think of is on offer! You can enjoy showing, showjumping, dressage, carriage driving and even endurance! Plus, the action's not just limited to the show's five arenas, as the endurance and driving competitors head out into the beautiful grounds surrounding the castle to put their horses through their paces.

FAST FACTS

Where: Windsor, Berkshire
When: 12-16 May
Why go: Non-stop equestrian action in the private grounds of Windsor Castle

DID YOU KNOW?

Windsor Horse Show was first held in 1943, and it was put on to raise money to help the war effort!

See the stars

Top riders from the world of dressage and showjumping will step into the main Castle Arena, hoping to take home one of the big prizes from the show! For showjumpers, the Grand Prix's the class they all want to win, while dressage riders strut their stuff in a bid to be crowned the winner of the Grand Prix and Grand Prix Special.

Drive time

The royal family has a passion for carriage driving, and it's one of the most popular attractions at Windsor. A highlight is always the driving Grand Prix, which is essentially eventing, but for horses pulling a carriage! First, competitors perform a driven dressage test, then they head out into the park for the marathon, where they drive at speed around eight obstacles. A cone driving test forms a thrilling finale, where the challenge is to drive between narrowly spaced pairs of cones within a set time.

The coaching marathon is another spectacular driving event. Coaches and horses step out into the park, with drivers and passengers decked out in period costume.

TOP TIP
Avoid getting stuck in a traffic queue by heading to Royal Windsor by train!

Show stoppers

Windsor's famous for its showing classes, too, and it's the perfect place to spot your favourite breeds! There are classes for natives, hunters and hacks, through to ex-racehorses, cobs and coloured horses and ponies.

Let me entertain you

As well as all the competitions, there'll be loads of epic displays and performances to entertain the crowds. Spectators have been wowed by the Shetland Pony Grand National, Pony Club mounted games and the musical ride of the Household Cavalry!

An enchanted evening

Windsor's famous for staging thrilling evening performances. The show has often included a theatrical pageant, showcasing the horse through the ages, and there have been displays, music and much more! As well as being a perfect way to spend a spring evening, you're sure to catch a glimpse of the castle lit up in the evening – which is simply breathtaking!

ALL THE INFO

To find out what's happening at this year's show, visit rwhs.co.uk

COMMON SENSE

Get to know your fave pony's sensitive side by learning all about his five senses

Finding out all about your fave pony's senses is a great way to help you understand how he interacts with the world around him. Just like you, he has five of them – sight, hearing, smell, touch and taste. They're all super-important and he uses them to explore his surroundings and keep himself safe. If you know how his senses work, it'll help you figure out how he's feeling and why he behaves the way he does.

DID YOU KNOW?

Ponies have a third eyelid that helps protect their eyes and keep them moist.

Watch out!

With his eyes positioned on the side of his head, your fave pony can see almost the whole way around his body. In the wild, this would make it super-easy for him to spot any predators before he ended up as their lunch!

Because of the way his eyes are positioned, a pony has two blind spots. He can't see directly in front or behind. If you watch your fave pony carefully, you might just see him turn his head to the side to get a better view of what's there.

As ponies are able to see so much more than you, he'll often spot stuff way before you notice it. This is why he might sometimes seem like he's spooking at nothing.

DID YOU KNOW?

Your fave pony has binocular vision, just like us, which means he can see the same image through both eyes. He also has monocular vision, so he can see separately through each eye, too.

Listen up

Ponies have much better hearing than us. Not only do they use it to listen to things around them, they can also figure out where a noise is coming from and what's making it. Their ears can turn 180°, which helps them hone in on a specific sound. With such super-sensitive ears, your fave pony can hear noises much sooner than you, too!

His ears can also show you how he's feeling. When he's happy or alert they'll point forward, but if something's bothering him they'll point backwards. If his ears are out to the side, he's probably listening closely for something.

DID YOU KNOW?

Your pony's ears help him keep his balance by letting his brain know how and where his head's positioned!

On the nose

Your fave pony uses his nose to sniff out food and identify other ponies, people and predators. His sense of smell's stronger than yours, but it's still not as powerful as a dog's.

He may use his nose to pick out scary or threatening smells, so if you're not sure why he's frightened, he might have caught a whiff of the vet visiting another pony on the yard, or the dog that often barks at him when you ride down the road.

Good taste

While your fave pony might not be a fussy eater, he'll still avoid poisonous plants while grazing – or that super-important medicine you put in his dinner! Ponies actively avoid bitter and sour tastes, and seem to prefer sweet or salty ones. Your fave pony's sure to appreciate the odd tasty treat (not too many, though!), but why not consider giving him a salt lick in his field or stable, too?

Can't stop the feeling

With super-sensitive skin, your fave pony can feel any change in your balance or seat while you're riding. Touch is also a really important way he socialises with his pals in the field. You might spot ponies nibbling each other's withers with their teeth. This is called mutual grooming, and they're helping each other out by scratching those hard-to-reach places and removing any loose hair. Giving your fave pony a scratch in his fave itchy spot is a great way to reward him and build a bond with him.

Know your pony

Tuning in to your fave pony's senses is the perfect way to understand his behaviour and strengthen the bond between you. Plus, the more time you spend with him, the more clues you'll pick up about how he's feeling and what he's thinking.

SIBLING >>> RIVALRY

Sisters Phoebe and Olivia don't see eye to eye when a new pony arrives

Sophia and Robin as
Phoebe and Mystic

Bella and Blue as
Olivia and Buzz

He's got to settle in first, Olivia. Don't you know anything?

Why does Phoebe have to be so mean, Buzz? She always thinks I don't know anything.

I can't wait to see what Mystic's like in the school.

He'll be much better than Buzz, that's for sure.

Hey, Buzz is an amazing pony.

Sure, he's fine for you, Olivia... but Mystic's deffo more advanced.

You're going to be such a good boy today, aren't you? I'm so excited!

Oh no! Where's my other boot gone?

THE CASPIAN HORSE

Discover the Caspian Horse's unique history

Elegant, refined and strikingly beautiful, the Caspian Horse may be small in stature, but it has an abundance of talent and personality, and was once the prized possession of Persian kings.

DID YOU KNOW?

The Queen's husband, Prince Philip, was involved in bringing the first Caspian Horses to the UK.

DID YOU KNOW?

Due to their calm, friendly nature, Caspian Horses are used for therapy and Riding for the Disabled Association sessions.

Standing tall

Despite only reaching a maximum height of 12.2hh, the Caspian's referred to as a horse, not a pony. This is because they're more like an Anglo Arab in build, conformation and movement than a pony. They're very elegant in the way they look and move, and have a floating action and smooth, rocking canter.

A Caspian would be a good contender if you're looking for a perfect Pony Club pony. Being small and narrow, it's an ideal mount for children and can turn a hoof to any activity, from jumping and dressage to eventing and showing. It makes a smart driving pony, too. Being light on its feet and extremely quick, the Caspian's also popular for mounted games, polo, and scurry and trials driving.

DID YOU KNOW?

Arabs and Thoroughbreds are believed to be descendents of Caspian Horses.

An incredible find

The Caspian originates from Northern Iran and has a fascinating history. It was believed to have been extinct for 1,000 years, before being rediscovered in 1965 by an American woman called Louise Firouz. She'd heard people talking about a small, narrow type of pony, and thought it sounded ideal for her young children. Louise set out to search for them, and was delighted to find they were the perfect children's riding pony she was looking for. She was so impressed she went on to set up a breeding herd.

Louise named the ponies after the Caspian Sea, as she discovered them close to it. She spent the rest of her life promoting the breed and working to secure its future.

A mystery solved

Louise's discovery of the Caspian Horse solved a mystery that had puzzled historians for many years. A small, fine horse had been depicted in many carvings and artefacts found in Iran, including those on the ruins of Persepolis, but it didn't resemble any known breed. The Caspian Horse proved to be the missing link in their research, and all the historical findings showed what an astonishing past the breed had enjoyed.

Looking to the future

Caspian Horses have fans all over the world, and have been exported to many countries since being discovered by Louise, including the UK and other parts of Europe, the US, Australia and New Zealand. However, despite its popularity, beauty and talents, the Caspian is very rare, and there are less than 2,000 in the world today.

Much is being done to secure a brighter future for these amazing ponies, however, and an international gene bank project has been established. Its aim is to prevent bloodlines dying out and to protect this incredible breed's unique characteristics for many years to come.

POLE-ISH your PONY'S PACES

Have a go at these epic polework patterns

POLEWORK TOP TIPS

- all these pole layouts can be ridden in trot, but you can start in walk to help show your pony what you want him to do

- ride the layouts on both reins, to make sure you work your pony evenly

- use poles that are all the same length, so your shapes are symmetrical and the striding's equal for your pony

- place your pole layout in the middle of the arena, so you've got plenty of space to work around it

DID YOU KNOW?

Polework can help improve your pony's performance in any discipline!

Schooling over funky pole layouts is really popular with loads of riders and it's easy to see why! It's awesome fun and makes sessions in the school way more interesting for you and your fave pony! Plus, working over and around poles has tons of benefits, and is a great way to help improve your fave pony's suppleness, balance, strength and responsiveness. It's not as complicated as it might look, and it's something anyone can try – all you need is a few poles!

TOP TIP
Why not try these exercises with your instructor first, so they can help you get the patterns and striding right?

Ride a transition in the box!

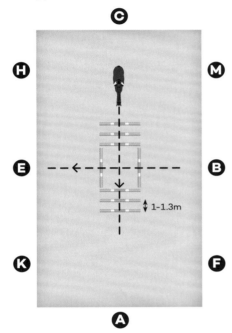

POLE PATTERN 1

All square
This is a super-simple layout that you can ride in several ways. It's especially good for helping with straightness and practising transitions.

Set it up
Use four poles to create a square. Then place two trotting poles in front of one side of the box, each 1-1.3m apart, depending on your pony's stride length. Place another two poles on the opposite side.

C
H   M
E ← B
↕ 1-1.3m
K   F
A

How to ride it
Option 1 Start by riding through the box, going in and out on the sides that don't have extra poles. You can try this in walk and trot.
Option 2 Do the same as option one, but use the box to make transitions. So, trot into the box, ride a walk transition, then exit over the pole in trot. Or, walk in, ask your pony to halt in the middle, then walk on again.
Option 3 Come down the centre line and ride over the trot poles, then continue through the box and ride out over the other poles.
Option 4 Take the same route as option three, but ride a transition to walk or trot in the centre square, then ride out of the box.

POLE PATTERN 2

In, out and round

You can easily create this layout by slightly adjusting the first exercise. It's great for working on circles, suppleness and straightness, too!

Set it up
Keep the square from your first pattern, but move the trotting poles so you have a pole at each corner of the box.

How to ride it
Option 1 As before, you can ride in and out of the square in any pace, and use it to practise transitions and square halts.
Option 2 Trot a circle around the box, going over each of the outer poles.
Option 3 You can adapt the circle exercise slightly by spiralling in and out. So, ride your circle over the corner poles, starting close to the outside edge. Then make the circle smaller, so you're getting closer to the square, before spiralling out again.
Option 4 Go in and out of the box and around and over the poles in a random pattern. It'll make sure your pony's listening to you, and is a great way to practise keeping him in a rhythm around a course of fences! You can try this in trot or canter.

❝ This is great for working on circles, suppleness and straightness ❞

POLE PATTERN 3

Criss-cross

Accuracy's super-important for riding, and this pattern will test your straightness and that you can guide your pony to exactly where you want him to go!

Set it up
You'll need six poles to create two triangles that touch at the tip.

How to ride it
Option 1 Start simple by riding over the very middle of the pattern, where the two triangles touch, to really test your straightness. You can approach on a straight line, or incorporate it into a circle.
Option 2 Go from the top of your criss-cross pattern to the bottom. You can do this in trot, but you may find it easier to stay straight if you start in walk.
Option 3 Ride a large circle that takes you through one of the triangles. Then change the rein and go the other way!

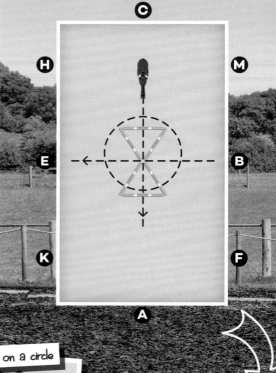

Practise your accuracy on a circle

POLE PATTERN 4

On the tri-angle

The gentle curve of this layout will help your pony develop correct bend through his body and he'll become super-supple, too.

Set it up
Use three poles to create a triangle, then place two trotting poles on either side, each 1-1.3m apart.

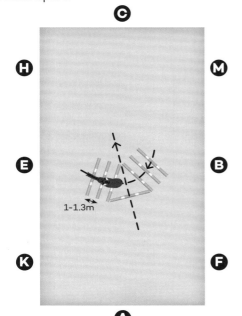

How to ride it
Option ❶ Ride from the top to the bottom of the triangle in either direction, to test your straightness. You can mix things up by adding in a transition as you enter or leave the shape.
Option ❷ Ride an arc over the trot poles and through the triangle. Aim for the very middle of each pole and encourage your pony to bend by opening your inside hand a little and using your inside leg on the girth and your outside leg behind the girth.

Test your straightness

Supple him up

THE SAND PONY

Freya's creation turned into something super-magical!

The sun was beating down onto the beach where Freya sat, right by the Caribbean sea. She was on holiday with her parents and younger sister, Sophie. Freya was excited to be in such a beautiful paradise, but felt slightly nervous, too. She didn't like the water, and wasn't a very good swimmer.

Making a masterpiece

While her mum laid in the sun, and her dad and Sophie went snorkelling, Freya spent hours drawing in the sand. She found a big stick, and traced the outline of a horse into the soft white sand. She made his long legs look as though they were galloping, then collected bits of seaweed to use as his flowing mane and tail. She decorated the rest of him with large seashells she'd found while splashing along the edges of the waves. Finally, she used a shiny black pebble as her pony's eye. Freya stood back and looked at her masterpiece with satisfaction, then grabbed her phone from her mum's beach bag to take a picture. He was perfect.

Dusk was falling, and most of the beach-goers had gone back to their hotels to get ready for dinner by the sea. "Freya," her mum called. "Time to go now." But Freya didn't want to leave just yet, as she worried her sand pony would be washed away by the tide. "Five more minutes?" she called back. Her mum shook her head and, reluctantly, Freya obeyed.

A surprise visit

All through dinner, Freya thought about her pony creation. She looked at the photo she took of him, her stomach knotting at the thought of him being gone when she returned the next morning. "Can I go back to the room, please?" Freya asked, hoping she might be able to sneak to the beach to check on him. "No, Freya. Not until everyone's finished," said her dad.

She went to bed that night thinking about the following day. Even if her sand pony had disappeared by the morning, at least she could spend the day

making another one. She drifted off to sleep but, not long after, she was woken by a tapping sound on the window. She froze, a little scared. Reaching for her phone and putting the torch on, she ventured over to the window to investigate. Their hotel room was on the ground floor, right next to the beach. Freya tentatively pulled back the curtains and gasped. There was a pony outside!

Come to life

Freya's stomach flipped as she looked at the golden pony standing proudly before her. He gave a snort, and she noticed a load of sand puff out of his nose. She pressed her hand up against the window and the pony met it with his nose. She could see his breath misting up the glass. "One sec," she whispered, before tiptoeing out of her bedroom, across the hallway and sneaking through the front door, trying not to wake her sleeping family.

It was still humid, even at night. She was running barefoot, but the sand slowed her down as her feet sank into it. Sure enough, the pony was standing there waiting for her. He almost blended into the background, as if wearing the perfect camouflage. When Freya ran up to him he snorted, but didn't seem scared. She got closer and noticed his mane was made of seaweed and, when she reached out to touch him, felt that his coat was made of sand. Her pony had come to life!

Journey to the sea

The sand pony flicked his neck to the side, as if indicating for Freya to jump onto his back. "But I've never ridden a pony before," she said. Sand Pony snorted again, trying to reassure her that everything would be okay. He moved over to a bench so Freya could climb up. As soon as she grabbed his mane, she felt completely secure, like some kind of magic was holding her on board. Sitting on his sandy back felt

> *As long as she held onto Sand Pony, she knew she was safe*

no different to sitting on the beach in the sun. Before Freya knew it, Sand Pony was galloping towards the ocean, and her stomach clenched with nerves. He plunged into the salty water and Freya took in a big gulp of air before they dove under the surface. As she looked around, she was sure she could see white horses made of foam, gallivanting amidst the waves.

Underwater adventure
They were completely submerged. Freya panicked at first that she wouldn't be able to breathe, but as long as she held onto Sand Pony she knew she was safe. The same magic that held her on seemed to be allowing her to breathe underwater, too. Sand Pony swam as fast as a dolphin, and lit up the water wherever he went. Even though it was dark, Freya was able to see all the fish and marine life around them clearly. She looked up towards the surface and saw a group of turtles paddling along. Beneath her were a couple of stingrays, gliding serenely above the ocean floor, while fish of rainbow colours circulated around in a tight-knit shoal. Freya had only ever seen things like this on the TV. She'd never even swam in the sea before now.

Eventually, Sand Pony turned back on himself and headed towards the shore. Freya stole one last look behind her, and could've sworn she glimpsed a long, silvery tail and mass of hair that looked like sea grass. She'd always remember it as catching sight of a mermaid.

Never forget
They broke the surface in a flurry of bubbles and sea foam. Freya took a deep breath in. She felt exhilarated. Sand Pony trotted through the surf the rest of the way and, as soon as they hit dry land, he felt bone dry as if nothing had ever happened. He walked back towards the hotel and, in that short time, Freya seemed to have dried off, too. She dismounted Sand Pony, suddenly feeling overwhelmed with tiredness. She gave him a big hug before trundling off to bed.

The next morning, Freya woke up feeling like it had all just been a vivid dream. She gulped down her breakfast and eagerly ran onto the beach, followed by her family, as soon as dawn broke. She scoured it in search of the Sand Pony, but he was nowhere to be found. "I'm sorry, Sweetie," her Mum said. "It was a lovely pony you drew in the sand. Why don't you make another one?" Freya sighed, staring at the sun while it rose above the horizon. "It's okay, Mum," she said. "He's back in the sea where he belongs."

"Why don't you come snorkelling with us today, Freya? We won't go very deep." Sophie chimed in excitely. Freya thought about it, remembering how amazing last night's adventure has been. "You know what, I think I will," she said, bringing her little sister in for a cuddle. "I thought you hated the water?" said her dad, suspiciously. Freya took out her phone and looked at the photo of Sand Pony that she'd treasure forever. "Actually, turns out it's not so bad after all."

How much do you ❤ PONIES?

Take our test to find out how big a pony fan you really are

Think you love ponies more than anything else in the whole wide world? Find out by taking our fun, super-quick test. Just tick all the statements that apply!

You always save the apple core from your lunch for your fave pony!

If your fave pony treads on your toe or dribbles green slobber over your gorgeous new riding top you forgive him straight away. ✓

Weekend lie-ins don't interest you. You want to get up and out to the yard as early as possible.

You've missed out on more than one party/sleepover/trip out with friends to go to a show, lesson or Pony Club rally – but you really didn't mind. ✓

You're always the first to volunteer for extra poo-picking – it's so worth it because you get to hang out with your fave pony for even longer. ✓

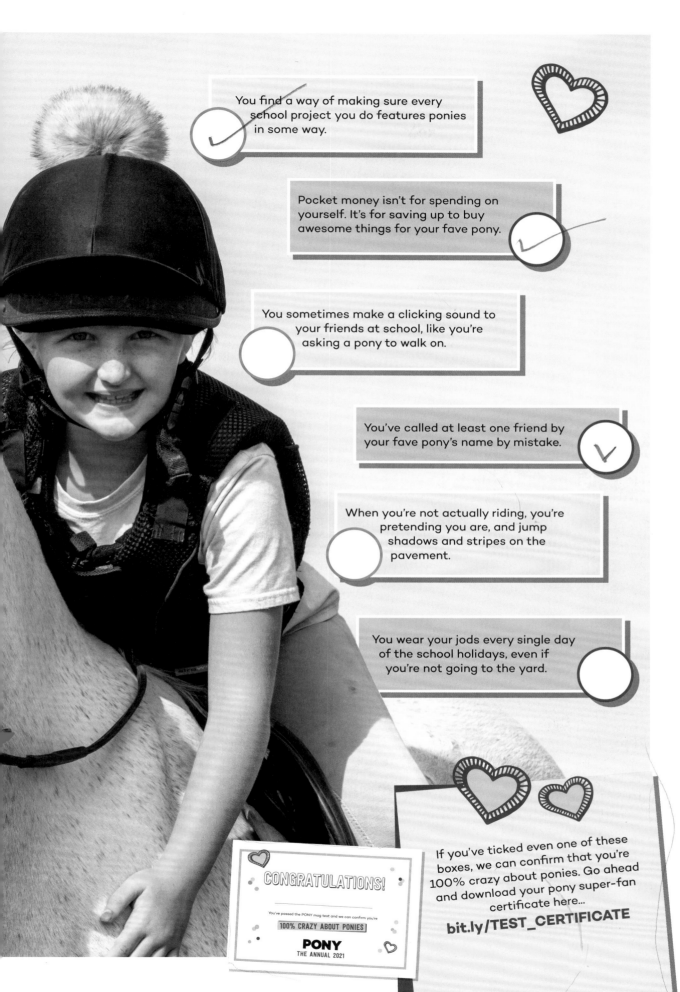

You find a way of making sure every school project you do features ponies in some way.

Pocket money isn't for spending on yourself. It's for saving up to buy awesome things for your fave pony.

You sometimes make a clicking sound to your friends at school, like you're asking a pony to walk on.

You've called at least one friend by your fave pony's name by mistake.

When you're not actually riding, you're pretending you are, and jump shadows and stripes on the pavement.

You wear your jods every single day of the school holidays, even if you're not going to the yard.

CONGRATULATIONS!

You've passed the PONY mag test and we can confirm you're

100% CRAZY ABOUT PONIES

PONY
THE ANNUAL 2021

If you've ticked even one of these boxes, we can confirm that you're 100% crazy about ponies. Go ahead and download your pony super-fan certificate here...

bit.ly/TEST_CERTIFICATE

KEEP YOUR PONY HAPPY

Discover everything your fave pony needs to keep him happy and healthy

TREATS

Doing all you can to make sure your pony stays content will mean he'll enjoy the time he spends with you even more, and it'll go a long way to keeping him healthy, too.

CUDDLES

Let's hang out

You probably don't need extra encouragement to spend loads of time with your fave pony, but being around him is the best way to learn about his likes and dislikes! It'll give you an insight into his normal, everyday behaviour, which means you'll easily be able to spot when something's not quite right with him.

When he's happy and well, your fave pony should be calm and relaxed, yet alert and interested in what's going on around him. He'll have a healthy appetite, and should be pleased to see you.

A pony who's not happy, or who feels ill or in pain, may appear stressed and anxious, or he may become depressed and be quieter than usual. He might lose interest in his food, could seem grumpier and not be so enthusiastic about being exercised.

If his behaviour does change in any way, it's important to call your vet and ask them to check him over.

LOVE

CARE

GRAZING GROOMING

CARROTS **FOOD** ROUTINE

FRIENDS HEALTHY

WATER SHELTER

SNOOZING EXERCISE

Here are all the things that are super-important for your fave pony...

1. Something healthy to munch on

Most ponies' fave thing ever is to eat, but they need to have the right amount and the right kind of food to stay healthy. Your pony should eat just enough to give him energy for his ridden work, and keep his body functioning. If he has too much, he's at risk of become overweight, and this could make him ill.

The most important thing he'll munch on is fibre, which can be grass, hay, haylage or chaff. As well as providing calories, fibre helps his digestive system work properly, and it also creates heat to keep him warm on cold days!

The best way to find out how much food he needs each day is to ask your vet or a qualified equine nutritionist for advice.

TOP TIP
Help your fave pony stay healthy by avoiding giving him too many sugary treats.

DID YOU KNOW?

Your pony will drink more on hot days, and also if he eats lots of dry food, such as hay in winter.

2. A refreshing drink

A cool drink of water will help refresh your pony on a hot summer's day, but it'll also help keep his food moving through his digestive system, so he doesn't get tummy ache. So, make sure he always has plenty of fresh, clean water in his buckets or trough, whether he's out in the paddock or in his stable. In winter, keep an eye on the weather, as you may need to break the ice on his water, so he can still drink.

3. Plenty of exercise

Ponies who live in the wild will be on the move for up to 18 hours a day! Our ponies might not need to walk so far, but it's still important that they get plenty of exercise. It'll help keep them slim, and it's healthier for their muscles and joints than standing around. It'll stop them getting bored, too.

4. Time outdoors

It's way better for ponies to be out in the fresh air, where they can move around constantly and hang out with their pony pals, than standing in a stable for long periods. Time in the paddock can help keep ponies chilled out, too, so they're calmer to ride.

If your pony puts on weight easily, or needs to lose a few pounds, it's important he doesn't eat too much grass, but there are ways to restrict how much he eats while he's outside. For example, you can use a grazing muzzle, strip graze the field or put him in a paddock that's already been eaten down by other ponies.

Of course, there are times when it can be a good thing to bring a pony inside for a short while, such as if the weather's bad, to get him away from pesky flies or help reduce his grass intake.

DID YOU KNOW?

When your pony moves around, the frog in his hoof helps pump blood around his body!

5. A secure routine

Ponies love knowing when they're going to be fed, or when they'll be turned out in the field with their pals, so try to set a routine that works for your pony and keep to it as best you can. He might start feeling stressed or anxious if he's kept waiting.

6. Friendly company

Ponies are herd animals, which means they're much happier when they're with their friends. As well as keeping each other company, they feel safer when they're not alone. If you watch ponies in the field, you'll notice they take turns to snooze while one stays awake and alert to look out for predators! Another thing ponies do for each other is scratch itches they can't reach! It's called mutual grooming and they'll use their teeth to scratch each other's withers, which also helps get rid of any loose hair or dead skin! You might see them using their tails to swish flies off each other in summer, too!

DID YOU KNOW?

If you're lucky enough to get a new pony or have one on loan, ask the previous owner about the pony's routine. Then you can follow it as closely as possible to help him settle in more easily.

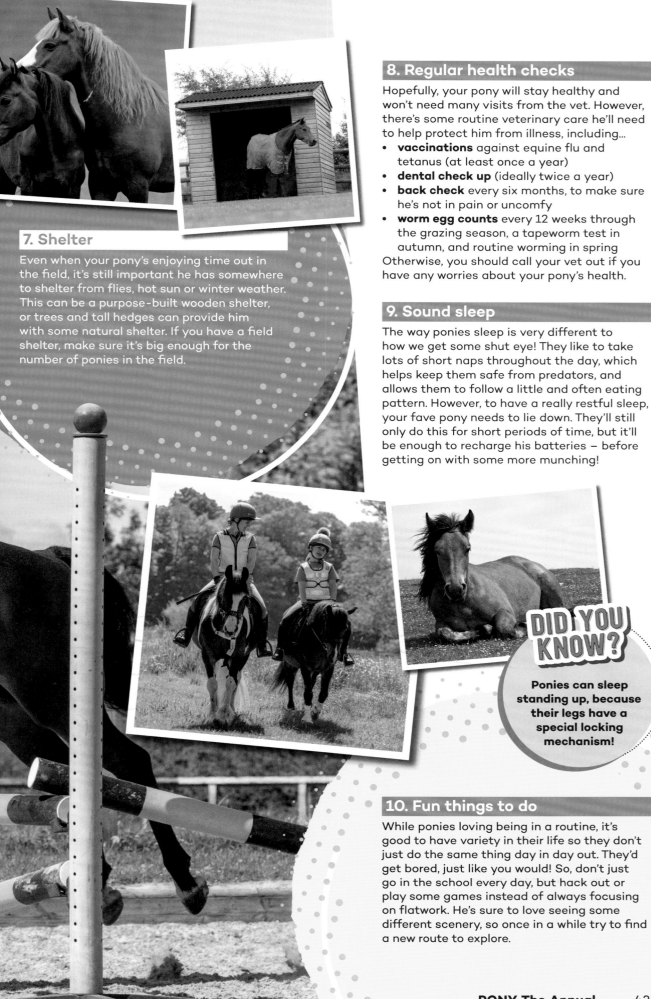

7. Shelter

Even when your pony's enjoying time out in the field, it's still important he has somewhere to shelter from flies, hot sun or winter weather. This can be a purpose-built wooden shelter, or trees and tall hedges can provide him with some natural shelter. If you have a field shelter, make sure it's big enough for the number of ponies in the field.

8. Regular health checks

Hopefully, your pony will stay healthy and won't need many visits from the vet. However, there's some routine veterinary care he'll need to help protect him from illness, including...

- **vaccinations** against equine flu and tetanus (at least once a year)
- **dental check up** (ideally twice a year)
- **back check** every six months, to make sure he's not in pain or uncomfy
- **worm egg counts** every 12 weeks through the grazing season, a tapeworm test in autumn, and routine worming in spring

Otherwise, you should call your vet out if you have any worries about your pony's health.

9. Sound sleep

The way ponies sleep is very different to how we get some shut eye! They like to take lots of short naps throughout the day, which helps keep them safe from predators, and allows them to follow a little and often eating pattern. However, to have a really restful sleep, your fave pony needs to lie down. They'll still only do this for short periods of time, but it'll be enough to recharge his batteries – before getting on with some more munching!

DID YOU KNOW?

Ponies can sleep standing up, because their legs have a special locking mechanism!

10. Fun things to do

While ponies loving being in a routine, it's good to have variety in their life so they don't just do the same thing day in day out. They'd get bored, just like you would! So, don't just go in the school every day, but hack out or play some games instead of always focusing on flatwork. He's sure to love seeing some different scenery, so once in a while try to find a new route to explore.

? QUIZ ?

GET SET AND VET

Ready to put your veterinary knowledge to the test? Have a crack at our pony health quiz!

Being savvy about pony health probs is super-useful because it can help you quickly spot if your own fave pony is unwell. Then you can make sure he gets the right help straightaway. You can test what you've learned so far by having a go at our fun veterinary quiz!

1. Why do you need to make changes to your pony's feed gradually?

A He might be allergic to the new food

B So his tummy can adjust to the new type of food

C To help him get used to the taste

DID YOU KNOW?

Your fave pony needs to eat at least 1.5% of his body weight in fibre every day!

2. How often should your fave pony be vaccinated against equine flu?

A Once every two years

B Once every five years

C At least once a year

3. Circle all the reasons you might need to put stable bandages on your pony.

A To make him look super-smart

B To protect a wound

C To reduce swelling when he's standing in the stable

D To stop his legs getting tired

E To protect his legs from bumps in the stable or while travelling

4. What signs might your pony show if he's suffering from azoturia (tying up)?

A He'll be stiff, feel sore and won't want to move

B He'll be full of energy and keen to run around

C He'll seem tired, but relaxed and interested in his food

7. What's the most suitable diet for a pony who's at risk of laminitis?

A Lots of treats and good-quality haylage

B A low-calorie balancer and soaked hay

C Competition nuts and sugar beet

8. How many teeth do adult ponies have?

A 36-44

B 26-34

C 70-75

5. How would you manage an abscess in your pony's hoof?

A Keep his foot really clean and put a poultice on it several times a day to help draw out the pus

B Leave it to heal by itself

C Bandage his legs every night

9. Which of these are signs that a pony might have colic?

A Sleeping a lot and eating but not drinking

B Rolling, kicking his belly and not wanting to eat

C Refusing jumps, not wanting to lie down and eating more hay than usual

Your fave pony's hooves are made of keratin, the same material your finger nails are made from!

Ponies can't vomit! This is why your fave pony's very particular about which parts of his paddock he grazes in, because if he eats something bad for him he can't get rid of it quickly.

6. Your fave pony's stomach is roughly the same size as a...

A Basketball

B Tennis ball

C Rugby ball

10. What might a pony with uveitis need to wear to help his condition?

A A fly or UV mask

B An extra rug in the winter

C A nose-net

Turn to p100 to find out how you got on!

FOALIN' AROUND!

Awww, there's nothing cuter than a gorgeous foal — here are some amazing facts about baby ponies!

A foal will be in his mum's tummy for 11-12 months before he's born.

Foals start off just drinking their mum's milk, but they'll begin nibbling grass within a few days of being born!

The first milk a newborn foal drinks is called colostrum. It's thick, yellow and sticky, and it's extra special because it contains antibodies to help the foal fight infections.

Want to know why foals always look like they've got super-long legs? Well, they're almost as long as they'll be when he's a fully grown horse! They just need to wait for his body to catch up with them!

A pony's called a foal for the first year of his life.

Sometimes twin ponies can be born, but it's really rare. Carrying two foals can put both the mum and the babies at risk.

Foals are often born at night, and this could be due to the fact that ponies are prey animals. Giving birth in the dark of night helps keep mum and baby safe from predators, and the little one will be up on his feet and ready to run by the time daylight arrives!

DID YOU KNOW?

Baby donkeys are called foals, too!

Plaits AMAZING!

How to create stunning plaits

Whether you want your fave pony to be smartly turned out for a show or you're planning to take an epic photo of him, plaiting his mane and tail will make him look amazing! Here's how...

KIT LIST

To plait up your fave pony you'll need...
- plaiting spray or water
- water brush
- mane comb
- plaiting bands or a needle and thread
- scissors
- a hair clip to hold the mane out of your way
- a sturdy box to stand on, to help you reach the higher parts of his mane

DID YOU KNOW?

While you won't get any extra marks for plaiting up for a dressage test, it'll give the judge a great first impression of you and your pony.

HOW TO... PLAIT A MANE

1. Divide your pony's mane up into equal sections, and fasten each bunch loosely with a plaiting band. This'll help make sure you get the right number of plaits, and that each one is roughly the same size.

2. Take one of the sections of mane, dampen it slightly with water or plaiting spray, then divide it into three smaller, equal sections. You can now begin plaiting, starting as close to your pony's crest as possible.

TOP TIP
It's usual to start plaiting from the top of the mane, but if your pony's fidgety you can start at his withers and work up instead.

3. Braid the section of hair all the way to the bottom. Hold the hair firmly as you plait to keep your work neat and tidy.

4. Secure the braid by wrapping a band around the bottom of it. Fold the ends of the hair under and wrap the band around once more to prevent any loose hairs poking out.

TURN OVER

TOP TIP
You can roll the plait up if you prefer – maybe have a go at both methods and see which you find easiest.

5. Fold the braid in half, then in half again, and secure the plait with another band.

6. Repeat all the way down your pony's mane to his withers, aiming to create plaits that are all the same size and evenly spaced.

7. Plait your pony's forelock. You can use the same method as the mane, or a French braid will look super-smart, too!

Sew cool

Using a needle and thread to secure your plaits will achieve a neater finish. They'll be less likely to come undone, but it'll take longer and can be more fiddly. You'll also need to be an ace at threading needles, and not be likely to drop them on the floor, or accidently poke your pony!

If you do choose to sew in your plaits, repeat the steps above, but sew the end of each long plait, then stitch the rolled or folded plaits in place.

TOP TIP
Ask a friend to help out by passing you the plaiting bands or threaded needles. It'll make your job much easier.

TA-DAH!

HOW TO... PLAIT A TAIL

A plaited tail looks totally awesome, and it isn't as tricky as you might think. Anyone can create a tail plait if they put in a little bit of practice! Here's how...

TOP TIP
If you're travelling your pony, pop a tail bandage on to protect your hard work.

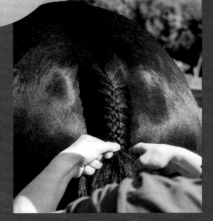

1. To prepare the hair, dampen it with a little water or plaiting spray. Then, starting at the very top of your pony's dock, take a little bit of hair from each side, and cross the left side over the right.

2. Take another small section of hair from the right and cross it into the middle. Then, do the same from the left, crossing it over so it joins the middle section.

3. Carry on down the tail in the same way, bringing in a small section of hair from each side as you go. Hold the hair firmly, to keep your plait neat.

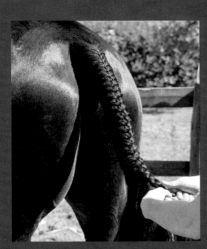

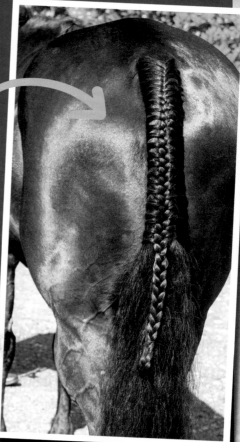

4. When you're approaching the end of your pony's dock, stop taking in any more hair from the sides, but continue plaiting.

5. Keep going until you've reached the end of the section of hair, then secure it with a band. Fold this long plait under, and fasten in place with another band, or sew it in for a neater look.

MEGA PONY PUZZLES

Have a go at our super-fun, pony-themed challenges

TACK TEASER

We've had a tack room tidy up and couldn't believe all the awesome pieces of kit that we discovered in there! You'll find some of them in our wordsearch!

U	L	B	A	N	D	A	G	E	S	S	D	B	K	J	G
S	H	U	E	L	A	G	N	I	T	R	A	M	N	O	R
H	T	G	N	F	O	H	A	O	S	O	T	I	A	A
G	X	O	I	G	S	C	B	E	O	E	E	E	L	U	S
R	U	R	O	E	E	L	R	P	B	E	Z	N	H	S	R
L	T	R	B	B	E	C	A	V	H	R	H	N	O	T	E
H	E	A	R	W	L	R	A	S	C	E	Y	O	N	I	I
B	N	A	R	E	T	E	E	V	A	S	X	B	E	R	N
D	R	A	D	S	L	S	V	D	E	S	F	R	R	R	S
Z	P	I	K	R	I	O	C	A	R	S	D	A	F	U	S
S	B	C	D	C	O	O	O	B	R	F	S	E	B	P	I
U	E	P	R	L	L	P	I	C	E	T	M	O	E	I	V
N	A	E	U	L	E	E	E	S	V	N	W	N	N	R	H
D	X	C	A	G	U	R	T	U	O	N	R	U	T	O	G
E	B	R	U	S	H	I	N	G	B	O	O	T	S	N	I
E	G	A	D	N	A	B	L	I	A	T	G	I	Q	S	H

Bridle
Brushing boots
Cooler rug
Ear bonnet
Exercise sheet

Girth
Headcollar
High vis

Martingale
Neckstrap
Noseband
Overreach boots
Reins
Stable wraps
Stirrup irons
Tail bandage
Travel boots
Turnout rug

ON THE FENCE

Prove you're a showjumping whizz by matching these different fences with their correct names!

2 ~~Water tray~~ wall

1 Planks

3 Water tray

5 Cross pole

4 Oxer

Cross-pole
Planks
Oxer
Wall
Water tray

SPOT THE DIFFERENCE

Look very carefully at these two pictures and see if you can find the eight differences between them!

HOW DID YOU GET ON?

Turn to p100 to check out the answers!

A

B

JUMP for FUN

Get set for a super showjumping practice sesh with our awesome exercises

Need some inspo for ways to improve your fave pony's showjumping skills? Then have a go at our super-fun exercises! You'll begin by getting your pony nicely warmed up over poles, then pop him over some simple grids to work on his rhythm, balance and suppleness!

TOP TIP
Before trying any of these exercises, make sure you've warmed your pony up on the flat in walk, trot and canter.

TOP TIP
You may need to adjust the distances slightly to suit your fave pony's stride length.

TOP TIP
If you're not sure how to set out any of these exercises yourself, ask your riding instructor or yard manager to help you.

EXERCISE 1

A winning warm-up

This is a really great way to begin a jumping sesh because it helps you think about your pony's rhythm, and it'll help supple him up, too!

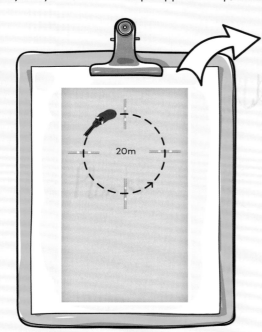

Set it up
Imagine a 20m circle is a clock face and place a pole on the ground at 12, 3, 6 and 9 o'clock. Position them slightly in from the track.

How to ride it
1. Begin by circling around the outside of all the poles, in trot.
2. Ride another circle, but this time choose one pole and trot over the middle of it. Go around the other three poles.
3. Continue this pattern, adding in another pole each time, until you're trotting over all four poles on the circle.
4. Change the rein and have a go the other way.
5. If your pony's finding it easy, try it in canter.

EXERCISE 2

Zig-zag poles
This trotting pole exercise will get your fave pony thinking about where he places his feet before you start jumping.

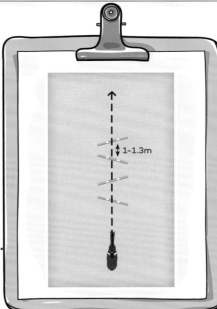

Set it up
Set out 4-6 poles, in a zig-zag pattern. The distance between each pole should be 1-1.3m, when measured from the middle.

How to ride it
1. Make sure your pony's trotting in a forward, energetic rhythm, then turn towards the line of poles.
2. Aim for the very middle of each one, and keep straight. Look up and ahead to help stop you wobbling!

Change it up
You can use this layout to ride different patterns. Ride over the first pole, then turn right and circle back over the third pole before looping round to the left and going over the fourth pole. You can even make up your own pattern that takes you over all of the poles!

EXERCISE 3

On the angle

When your pony's got the idea of the zig-zag poles you can try a similar exercise with jumps! It'll teach you how to ace fences on an angle to save time in a jump-off!

Set it up

Build three low, easy fences that are on a slight angle to each other. They should be one canter stride (approx 6m) apart, measured from the very middle.

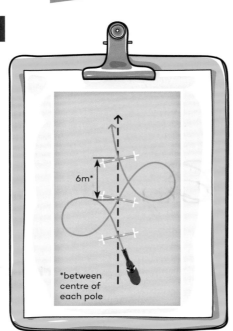

6m*

*between centre of each pole

How to ride it

1. Introduce your pony to each fence by jumping them one at a time. So, go over fence one, then head straight ahead before looping back round and popping over fence two. Land and turn back to fence three.
2. Next, aim to jump through the line of three fences, straight down the middle. You'll be jumping each one on an angle, so use your legs and reins to help keep your pony super-straight. Remember to look up and ahead, too, to stop you wobbling.

Change it up

Practise your jump-off turns by riding through the first pattern in the quickest time possible! You could also challenge your friends to see if they can beat your time!

EXERCISE 4

I ♥ ponies

Show your pony how much you love jumping – and him – by riding through this fun, heart-shaped grid!

Set it up

Place three fences down the middle of the arena, one canter stride apart (approx 6m). Then build two single fences to the left and right side of the school, just above the first fence. They should be slightly angled (see diagram).

How to ride it

1. Jump through your grid of three fences, then continue straight for two strides before riding a smooth turn to the right.
2. Curve round to pop over your single fence, then go large around the arena and approach the grid again.
3. This time, turn left after going through the grid and jump the single fence on that side.
4. Keep your pony guessing by mixing up which way you turn.

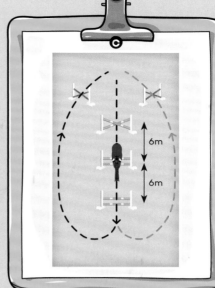

6m
6m

Show your pony how much you love jumping

EXERCISE 5

On the bounce
A bounce is where your pony lands after a fence, then takes off again for the next one straightaway. It's something anyone can have a go at, just keep the fences low and easy to start with.

Set it up
Place two low cross-poles approx 3m apart. To help you get a good approach, use a placing pole on the ground 2.7m before the first fence.

How to ride it
1. Make sure your pony has lots of energy in his canter, then approach the bounce. Wrap your legs around his sides to encourage him forward, sit up with your shoulders back and have an even contact on the reins.
2. You can fold a little as he takes off over the first fence, but don't get too far forward or he'll find it harder to push off the ground to jump the second fence.
3. Your pony might be surprised by the bounce at first, so ride through it two or three times until he's comfortable with what he's doing.

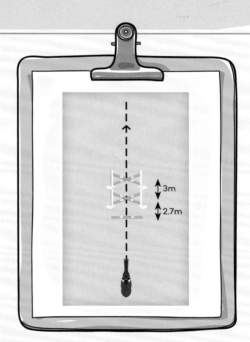

3m
2.7m

Change it up
If your pony's finding this easy, add another bounce! To do this, build a third cross-pole, 3m from the second fence. You can also raise the cross-poles to small uprights.

Flying finish
Practising these exercises regularly will make jumping sessions even more awesome! Plus, it'll help improve all the things you need to ace a showjumping course, such as straightness, rhythm, balance and accuracy!

ALL THE COLOURS

Get clued up about pony coat colours and markings

MARKINGS

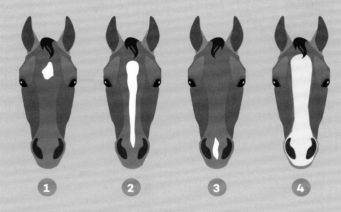

1. **Star** – a white patch between the eyes
2. **Stripe** – a narrow strip of white down the face
3. **Snip** – a white patch between the nostrils
4. **Blaze** – a wide white strip down the face
5. **Socks** – white on the leg that runs from the coronet band to just above the fetlock or below the knee
6. **Stockings** – white hair from the coronet band up to or above the knee

COLOURS

Grey

These can be iron, fleabitten, rose or dappled

Bay

A light or dark brown body with a black mane and tail, and dark hair on the lower legs

Tri-coloured

Bay, brown and black

DID YOU KNOW?

A truly white pony will be born white and stay that way for the rest of his life, while grey ponies' coats change colour as they age.

Chestnut

Comes in a variety of shades, from bright to liver

Palomino

A golden coat with a light mane and tail, often with white socks or stockings

DID YOU KNOW?

Blue roan ponies are sometimes mistaken for greys. However, while grey coats lighten with age, roans don't.

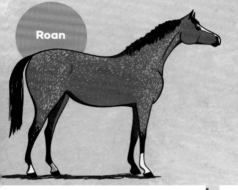

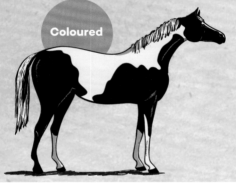

Roan

Can be blue, bay or strawberry

Coloured

Used to describe a piebald, which is black and white, or skewbald, which is white with any other colour, but usually brown

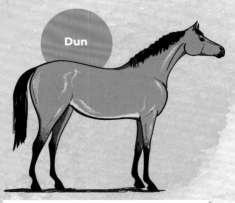

Black

A dark coat colouring all over the body, without any different shades on the legs

Dun

A sandy brown colour with black points (mane, tail and legs), much like a bay

DID YOU KNOW?

A true dun has a dorsal stripe. This is a dark strip along his spine. If a pony's dun coloured but doesn't have a stripe, it means he's actually buckskin.

MY SECRET YARD

Lydia always dreamed of running her own yard. When she found the perfect place hidden away, she could hardly resist...

For as long as I could remember, I've wanted to be just like Laura, the yard manager at my riding stables. She's super-cool, an out-of-this-world rider and knows EVERYTHING about ponies! She organises the best lessons, lets me help out at the yard and even offered me a beautiful chestnut pony, Cindy, to loan once. I'd begged my parents, but they said I wasn't old or responsible enough... yet!

It's my ultimate dream to run a yard of my own one day and be a mega-inspiring instructor – as well as have my own pony, of course! So, when my best friend, Madison, and I stumbled across the most amazing secret place on our walk home from school one afternoon, I thought my dream might be a little bit closer to coming true...

A different path

It was a glorious summer's day, so Madison and I decided to walk home across the footpath that ran through the fields, instead of going through the village. We were chatting away, enjoying the smell of wildflowers and the gentle humming of insects in the air. Suddenly, Madison stopped.

"What's up, Maddie?" I asked. "They've cut some trees down over there," she replied, pointing. "What about the wildlife that lives in them?" As I looked closer, something caught my eye. "Look, Maddie, I think there's a house behind those trees." She stared at where I was pointing. "How odd," she said. "They can't have built it recently. It must've been there this whole time, hidden by the trees."

I suddenly felt the urge to explore. "Come on," I said. "Let's check it out." Madison was unsure at first and tried to call me back, but I'd already run off across the field excitedly.

The magical discovery

When we reached the newly chopped trees, we could see the house up close. It was built of grey stone with enormous windows. There was a huge front door which had been painted red, but the colour had clearly started to peel off some time ago. We guessed the house must be super-old.

But, set back a little further from the house, there was a stable block! I couldn't believe it. Madison and

> **We pretended it was our very own yard, where we had to care for the ponies**

I rushed over to get a closer look. We discovered five brick stables, covered in cobwebs, but definitely in usable condition.

"Wow!" I squeaked. "Imagine living here and having your own ponies in these stables."

"I wonder why it's been abandoned?" mused Madison. "It's the most perfect place ever."

"Well the place clearly hasn't been lived in for years, so surely no one will mind if we play in the stables?"

New favourite place

Madison and I went to the stables, which we named Honeysuckle Grove, every day after school. We pretended it was our very own yard, where we cared for the ponies and taught riding lessons. We even found some old brooms to tidy the place up with.

One day I said to Madison: "What if we brought some actual ponies down here? That'd make it feel so much more real!"

"I'm not sure, Lydia," she replied. "I don't think it would be right. Laura trusts us to take the ponies out hacking and bring them back safely, not mess around at a yard that isn't even ours!"

"But it *feels* like ours!" I snapped, "Come on, Maddie. It'll be totally fine. No one's ever told us off for being here, have they?"

Reluctantly, Madison agreed, and we planned to bring the ponies over the very next day.

Our Honeysuckle ponies

Madison and I met at the riding school. I tacked Cindy up, my dream chestnut mare, and Madison got Poppet ready, a little piebald cob.

"Going out for a ride girls?" Laura popped her head out of the office.

I was startled. "Yeah, we'll be back in a couple of hours. I've got my phone on me."

Laura smiled. "Perfect. Have fun and stay out of trouble!"

I felt really bad that we hadn't told Laura where we were going, but I soon forgot about it when we trotted up the drive to Honeysuckle Grove. We dismounted, untacked the ponies and put them in the stables we'd cleaned. It made such a perfect picture!

We began to play mucking out until, all of a sudden, we heard a car crunching up the drive. We froze.

Rumbled!

I peeped my head over the stable door. It was a police car! My blood went cold. Had Madison and I done something really wrong?

A police officer stepped out of the car. "Come out, I know you're there!" she called. Madison and I obeyed, and tip-toed out of the stables.

"Now, girls," said the police officer. "You do realise you're trespassing?"

I gulped. I didn't even know what that meant, but it sounded pretty bad.

"It means you've gone onto someone else's land without permission," she continued.

"I'm so sorry," I mumbled. "We didn't think it belonged to anyone. We didn't realise we were doing anything wrong."

"It's been abandoned for some time, but it's recently been bought by someone," said the police officer. My heart sank. She carried on: "I'm sure it was just a misunderstanding. Now, I assume these ponies belong to you both?"

My heart sank even further. "No, they don't," said Madison in a very quiet voice. "They belong to our yard manager. She let us hack them out for her."

The police officer raised an eyebrow. "I think I'm going to have to give her a call and let her know where her ponies have got to. And your parents should know what you've been doing, too."

The police woman made a few calls, and Laura soon arrived with the horsebox to take Cindy and Poppet home. Mum also came to pick Madison and I up. We both felt awful. How were we going to make it up to them? And who had bought Honeysuckle Grove?

Making amends

We hurriedly explained everything to our parents and Laura – how we'd never meant any harm, and how we'd fallen in love with Honeysuckle Grove. We didn't think we were doing anything wrong by being there, but we understood now what trespassing was, and that it was against the law – for people and ponies!

Laura forgave us, but we weren't allowed to hack out alone for a little while after. Things did go back to normal in the end, but we really missed our afternoon trips to Honeysuckle Grove.

A happy ending

One sunny Saturday, I was on a walk with my parents when we went past Honeysuckle Grove. I hung my head, but Dad got some keys out of his pocket. "I suppose this is a good time to welcome you to your new home." I did a double take. It turned out the mystery buyers were Mum and Dad! They hadn't known about my trips here with Madison before they bought it, but when they found out, they'd kept it a secret to teach us a lesson! They'd decided to move somewhere bigger with room for a pony – because I now have Cindy on loan, and she lives at Honeysuckle Grove!

I've definitely learned my lesson, but I couldn't be happier to be living at my secret yard!

EVENTS

CHATSWORTH
HORSE TRIALS

Why a trip to Chatsworth Horse Trials makes a perfect weekend for all the family

The Dodson & Horrell Chatsworth International Horse Trials takes place every spring, and is held in the beautiful Derbyshire countryside. As well as offering top-level eventing action for riding fans, there's something for the whole family to enjoy, too!

Andrew Nicholson is a previous winner

Roll of honour

Chatsworth attracts the world's top riders, and previous winners include Oliver Townend, William Fox-Pitt, Andrew Nicholson, Piggy March and Mary King!

An eventing spectacular

The event has so much going on and, because there are several different levels of competition, you'll be spoilt for choice! One of the key highlights is that you can watch cross-country action on both Saturday and Sunday. It really is the perfect destination for eventing fans.

Down by the river

Chatsworth also has a popular arena eventing competition, which is open to amateur riders! It runs on the Friday and Saturday, and the classes are for BE90 and BE100 levels. It's held in a picturesque spot by the river, where riders tackle a course of showjumps before heading out onto the cross-country course. It's the ideal place to enjoy a picnic while watching the action!

Fun for all

Aside from the eventing, there's non-stop fun for all at Chatsworth. You can watch exciting demos and displays, from falconry to scurry driving, and there's loads of children's activities on offer, too, including face painting and crafts. Plus, you can browse the enormous shopping village and take home some awesome goodies.

TOP TIP

If your family has a dog, why not take him along and enter the fun dog show or have a go at agility?

Master of ceremonies

Chatsworth is one of six events that make up the Event Rider Masters series. Designed to make top-level eventing even more exciting, it condenses the three disciplines into two days. To keep everyone gripped to the very last minute, the riders do their cross-country round in reverse order, with the highest placed rider going last. Plus, spectators are treated to a lively commentary, which helps make the event highly entertaining!

Where it's at

The horse trials are held in the grounds of Chatsworth House near Bakewell, home of the Duke and Duchess of Devonshire. The magnificent house and beautiful gardens are open to the public, and with amazing works of art, water features, sculptures, a maze and adventure playground, there's loads to entertain non-horsey family members while you enjoy the main event!

ALL THE INFO

Check out chatsworth.org/events/horse-trials for the lowdown on the 2021 event!

AMERICAN MUSTANG

Discover the USA's fab feral horses

The majestic Mustangs of America are beautiful, fast and athletic. You'll find them galloping through canyons in massive herds, wild and free. Aside from looking super-stunning, they have lots of unique characteristics and strengths, too. Find out why Mustangs are so spectacular!

FACT FILE
Height: 14hh-16hh
Colour: Bay, sorrel, chestnut and paint
Known for: Being agile, fast and sensitive

Place of origin: USA

Perfect presence

Mustangs are super-lovely to look at, as they're perfectly in proportion and have floaty paces. They have a long, high-crested neck and muscular, sloping shoulders. The easiest way to recognise a Mustang is by his head, which is narrow and fine.

They're nimble and built for speed due to their long, fine legs. They also have compact hooves, and a low set tail.

Back to their roots

When the Spanish explorers discovered America in the 16th century, they brought over some of their Spanish horses with them. The horses were cross-bred with other breeds over time, commonly with Quarter horses and draught horses, to create the Mustangs we know today.

A lot of people call Mustangs the wild horses of America but, because they're descended from domestic horses who had escaped, they're actually feral.

DID YOU KNOW?

In times of danger, different herds of Mustangs have been known to team up together so they seem more intimidating!

Born free

Mustangs can be found grazing on grassland areas in the Western states of America. They're allowed to run free across 34 million acres of public land – wow!

They live in big herds, usually consisting of a stallion, around eight mares and their foals. If in danger, it's the alpha mare's job to lead the herd to safety if a predator tries to attack, while the stallion stays and puts up a fight.

Making friends

Some Mustangs are domesticated and used for riding. They make great hacking horses because of their sure-footedness and sturdy legs. They're also super-fast and agile, which means they can do a lot of different disciplines, such as racing, endurance and even showing.

Mustangs can bond very deeply with a human once they learn to trust them. They can be hard to train at first, though, as they're very independent, and they're really good at picking up on a human's emotions, too.

TOP TIP
To go the extra mile, why not ask your guests to arrive dressed as unicorns? They could wear a unicorn onesie or headband!

GET THE PARTY STARTED

Plan a pony-tastic sleepover!

Want to throw an awesome sleepover party for you and your pony-mad friends? We've got lots of super-fun ways to make sure you have a totally awesome time, with tons of horsey activities to try!

1. Ponyfy your room

Set the scene by turning your room into a pony-themed wonderland! Start the party right by sending your guests adorable pony-styled invites. Then, ask them to help you design some pony bunting to hang up when they get there! Add some streamers and pony pics on the wall for the finishing touch!

*Dear..........
You are invited to my pony sleepover party*

2. Make pony snacks

You're sure to feel a little peckish during all your sleepover activities! To keep with your pony theme, why not make a few horsey snacks to munch on with your friends? You could bake horseshoe biscuits, unicorn cupcakes or even make a pizza in the shape of a pony!

Ask an adult for help when using the oven and handling hot cakes and pans.

3. Make magical masks

Get into the pony spirit by creating super-cute unicorn masks to wear! All you need is some paper, scissors, elastic, colouring pencils and some glitter glue! Mask making's an awesome activity to do when your guests arrive – plus you'll all look super-cute!

TOP TIP
If you make your mask out of thick card instead of paper, it'll be extra robust and look even better!

6. Host a horsey fashion show

Walk the runway in your best pony gear! Ask your friends to bring a couple of their fave jods, tops and even a show jacket so you can take it in turns to parade along the catwalk. There's nothing more fun than giving each other a pony makeover to look just like a pro rider!

TOP TIP
Why not mix things up and swap some of your friends' outfits around to create new ones? The possibilities are endless!

Set the scene by turning your room into a pony-themed wonderland!

4. Play a horsey game

Keep your guests entertained by playing some awesome games! If it's a warm summer evening, why not head into the garden and play unicorn horn ring toss, or even a game of tag while pretending you're ponies! If you're staying inside, get out a pony board game or create a quiz to test your friends' pony knowledge!

7. Have a movie marathon

What better way to chill out with your mates than to gather round and watch your fave pony flick. There are so many great horsey films to choose from – try putting it to a vote to decide which one you watch. Or, even better, the prize for one of your pony games could be that the winner gets to choose the film. Don't forget to make some popcorn, too!

5. Personalise your pillowcases

If you feel like getting crafty, ask your guests to bring with them an old white pillowcase they can decorate. Provide a few sets of coloured fabric markers and get drawing! See who can come up with the best horsey design, and don't forget to include a drawing of your own fave pony on there!

ALL SQUARE

Find out how to master a super-square halt!

Being able to ride a square halt will earn you loads of marks in a dressage test, and it'll really impress the judge in a showing class, too. Here are five great tips to help you ace it!

10 OUT OF 10

For a great halt, your pony should stand square with equal weight in all four feet, so he's in perfect balance. His forelegs should line up with his hindlegs and you want his body to be super-straight, with his head facing forwards.

TOP TIP

If you're not lucky enough to have mirrors in your school at home, ask a friend to watch you and let you know when your pony's standing correctly.

TOP TIP

If you're going from trot to halt, don't expect your pony to stop immediately. It's fine if he takes one or two steps of walk before halting.

1. DO IT ON THE REGULAR

The best way to get to grips with halts is to ride loads of them! Don't just save them for flatwork sessions – you can include halt practice in jumping sessions, and they're really easy to do out on a hack, too! The more you do, the easier they'll become.

2. AIM FOR PERFECTION

If you always ask your pony to halt correctly, it'll become second nature to him and he'll soon stand square every time. So, be super-consistent and, if it's not perfect, give him a gentle nudge with your leg to encourage a trailing hindleg forward, or to move his quarters over.

3. THINK FORWARD

It may sound a bit odd, but to ride a great halt you need your pony to have lots of energy! It's important to keep riding forward into your downward transition, rather than pulling up quickly or just letting him fall into the halt. So, make sure you have a soft, even contact on your pony's mouth and keep your legs wrapped around his sides. Let him know you want him to halt by gently squeezing the reins, then put a little more weight into your seat and stop the movement of your hips.

4. SUPPORT HIM WITH YOUR POSITION

Your pony won't be able to perform a good halt if you're not in balance, so double check your riding position. Make sure you're sitting evenly with equal weight in both seat bones, and sit up straight with your shoulders back. Don't forget to keep looking up and ahead, too!

5. TAKE A BOW

Don't throw away valuable marks by riding an awesome halt, then saluting to the judge in the wrong way! Wait until your pony's standing still before you salute, then take both reins in one hand, and gracefully lower your free arm to your side. Nod your head, then retake your reins. It's important to remember that you can use your left or right arm to salute, but it should not be the hand you carry your whip in.

QUIZ
CARE PACKAGE

Test your knowledge by helping Eve care for her new pony, Twilight

Eve's dream pony, Twilight, has just arrived at the yard! It's her first time owning a pony, and she's asked you to help her care for him so he has the best life ever!

1. What questions should Eve ask Twilight's previous owner to help him settle into his new home?

A Is he fast out on a hack?

B What daily routine is he used to, and what feed does he have?

C Does he like being groomed?

2. Twilight has to be kept away from the other ponies for his first three weeks at the yard. Why's this?

A To make sure he doesn't have any infectious diseases that could spread to the other ponies

B Because he might distract the other ponies while they're being ridden

C So Eve can have some special bonding time with him

DID YOU KNOW?

Keeping a pony's vaccinations up to date will help stop him getting ill.

3. Twilight's previous owner said he's prone to sweet itch in the summer months. Which rug will help protect him?

A A stable rug

B A turnout rug

C A fly rug

4. Eve's decided to ride Twilight on their first hack! Where would be best to take him, and who should she go with?

A She should ride along quiet country lanes or a bridleway, with a reliable and quiet pony as a companion

B She should take him to the gallops with three of her friends

C She should venture off down a new track all by herself

DID YOU KNOW?

Giving your pony a daily groom will help his coat stay in good condition.

5. Which tool should Eve use to muck out Twilight's straw bed?

A A shavings fork

B A four-pronged manure fork

C A rake

6. Twilight's allowed to meet his new field buddies! What's the best way for Eve to introduce them?

A Let them get to know each other by putting them in neighbouring paddocks for a few days

B Put him straight in with them and hope they all get on well

C Let them touch noses over the stable door first

7. Eve wants to give Twilight a pamper sesh. Which brush is best to use to remove dust from his coat?

A Metal curry comb

B Face brush

C Body brush

8. It turns out Twilight's very greedy! How can Eve stop him eating up his hay so quickly?

A Put it in a small-holed haynet

B Put it in a bucket

C Spread it out all over the stable floor

9. Twilight has a full set of shoes, so how often should Eve book the farrier?

A Once every few months

B Every six to eight weeks

C Every four weeks

10. Eve's going to have a jumping lesson on Twilight, but what boots should she put on to protect his legs?

A Tendon boots

B Turnout boots

C Travel boots

Turn to p100 to find out how you got on!

TAKE THE LEAD

Be super-savvy around ponies

Knowing how to handle a pony on the ground's a really useful skill to have. It'll help you stay safe, and improve your confidence around ponies, too. Here's what you need to know...

Follow the leader

You're sure to spend more time with your fave pony on the ground than you do riding him, which makes handling him correctly so important. There are loads of things you'll need to do with him, such as leading him to and from his paddock, grooming him, picking out his feet and loading him into the trailer.

If you ride at a riding school, you may be asked to lead the pony back to his stables after your lesson, or there might be a chance to help with yard chores sometimes.

DID YOU KNOW?

Spending lots of time with your pony on the ground will help you build a strong bond with him.

Kit list

Wearing the right safety kit's just as important for leading your fave pony as it is for riding him. You should always wear your riding hat, with the chinstrap fastened, in case he accidently bumps into you. Pop your riding gloves on to protect your hands, too, in case he pulls on the rope.

Your riding boots are the ideal footwear for the yard, as they'll offer some protection to your feet if he steps on them. Soft shoes, such as trainers or flip-flops, won't offer any protection at all, so never wear them around ponies.

TOP TIP

Ask your riding school if they'll put on some stable management sessions, so you can practise your leading skills.

How to lead correctly

1. Stand on your pony's left side, close to his shoulder. Place your right hand on the leadrope just below the clip, with your knuckles facing forward. Then take the rest of the rope in your left hand. The leadrope shouldn't drag on the ground. If it's too long, fold the end over and hold the doubled-up section.

2. Ask your pony to 'walk on' and step forward. If he's used to being led, he should move with you. If he doesn't, it's something you'll need to practise. It's best to do this somewhere safe and enclosed, such as the arena, and ask someone experienced to help you.

3. Stay at your pony's shoulder as you both walk along. This is the safest position to be in, and helps you stay in control. Don't get in front of him, or let him overtake you.

4. To turn around, always move your pony away from you, so you'll be turning him to the right. This gives him more room to make a balanced turn, and it'll help avoid him stepping on you, too.

BE SAFETY SAVVY
Always be super-careful when holding a leadrope, and don't wrap or loop it around your hand or fingers. If your pony pulls away suddenly, this could cause a nasty injury.

TURN OVER

Trot on

It's a good idea to practise trotting your pony up in-hand, too. This will be super-useful if you plan to compete in any showing classes, as you may need to run him up in front of the judge. It's also handy in case you're asked to trot him up for the vet, perhaps if they want to check whether or not he's lame.

Just like when you make a transition from one pace to another when you're riding, you want your pony to step up from walk to trot as soon as you give him the signal. You should be able do this just by moving up into a jog yourself. Again, this may take a little bit of practice, and it can help to give him a voice aid to let him know what you want him to do.

You want your pony to step up from walk to trot as soon as you move into a jog yourself

Turnout tips

Going into the field can be super-exciting for ponies! There's all that fresh grass to munch, and friends to run around with, too. This means you'll need to take extra care when turning him out.

Once you're in the field, turn him around so he's facing the gate. That way you can close it to stop him escaping! Then move away from the gate, but turn him to face it again before you remove his headcollar. This gives you more time and room to step away before he races off!

TOP TIP
Giving your pony a treat as you slip off his headcollar can teach him to wait politely, instead of rushing off straightaway.

TOP TIP
Always be on the look out for any safety hazards around the yard, and let the owner or manager know straightaway if you spot something.

TOP TIP
If your pony's strong to handle, consider leading him in his bridle.

Quietly does it

Even the most well-behaved pony can be spooked by a sudden movement. Always be calm and quiet around ponies, and it's especially important not to run, or even walk, up behind them. The correct and safest way to approach is to move towards his shoulder, and always talk to him so he knows you're there. When you're close enough, stroke or pat his shoulder or neck as a friendly "hello".

If you want him to lift his leg so you can pick out his feet, start by placing your hand on his shoulder or hindquarters. Then run your hand slowly down to his fetlock, before giving it a squeeze to give him the signal that you want him to lift it up.

Speak his language

Your pony can let you know how he's feeling through his body language, so always keep an eye on his face, especially his eyes and his ears, when you're leading or handling him. If you spot any signs of fear or tension, you can reassure him or turn him away from whatever it is that's worrying him.

FUN WITH FLAGS

When Izzie and Bella can't get to a mounted games rally, they decide to hold their very own practice sesh!

Emily as **Izzie**

Melissa as **Bella**

Bonnie as **Lacey**

Bad news girls... the lorry won't start. I'm not sure we can go to the rally now.

What!

The mechanic doesn't think he'll get here in time, and it's too late to ask for a lift from someone. I'm really sorry.

Hang on... maybe we don't have to miss out!

What do you mean?

ON THE YARD....

I'm sure I've seen some stuff in the shed. We could use it to hold our own mounted games rally!

Oh, I see!

So, you pick up the flag and pass it to the next rider. Then they race down and put it in the cone.

It sounds tricky, Bella. I'm not sure I can do that!

A FEW MINUTES LATER...

I've just had an idea. Instead of riding, I can be your trainer!

That would be great, Bella. I'll go tack up Lacey!

FESS UPS

Read the cringey confessions of riding school ponies!

On the wrong foot

My rider, Melanie, came over to collect me from my stable, ready for her riding lesson. She started leading me over to the school, but stopped to chat to her friend on the way. After a while I got a bit impatient and started fidgeting. Suddenly I heard a yell, so I looked around with my ears pricked in surprise, wondering what was going on. Then I looked down and saw that I was standing on Melanie's toe! Oops! She was okay when I moved it off though.

Bailey

Jumping Jack

The other ponies and I were being asking to trot over some poles, and this made me feel excited. When it was my go, I jogged up to them, champing at the bit and struggling to contain myself. When I got to the first one I leapt over it as if it was a massive fence! Luckily my rider didn't fall off, but afterwards I felt a bit silly as the other ponies were going over them as if they weren't even there!

Jack

Puddle trouble

I was in a lesson with one of my regular riders, Erin. It'd been raining so the school had a few puddles in, and I'm not a big fan of water. Luckily we were avoiding the worst of them, until Erin asked me to canter. We approached one of the puddles and she didn't appear to be steering me away so I thought I'd do it for her. I darted to the side and carried on cantering, until I noticed that I'd left her behind! She'd landed right in the puddle, but thankfully just laughed it off!

Lily

All talk

After a great lesson in the arena, I was grazing in the field with my mates. I kept boasting about how much better I was at jumping than them, so they dared me to prove it to them by jumping a fallen tree branch in the field. I said I obviously could, but tried to make an excuse not to as I was a bit scared really. They wouldn't let it go, so I agreed to show them. I cantered up to the fallen tree, but stopped and ran out at the last minute. My friends couldn't stop laughing at me and I felt very silly for boasting!

Reggie

WHOOPS!

KINDA CRINGE

SOOOO CRINGE!

CRINGE-O-METER

Greedy guts

While waiting in my stable for my first rider of the day, I noticed my door wasn't shut properly. I decided to push it with my nose and, sure enough, it opened. I couldn't believe my luck and made a beeline for the hay barn. I crammed as much hay into my mouth as I could, and it tasted delicious! After a while, there was a voice coming towards the barn. It was the instructor who'd come looking for me! I was caught red handed stuffing my face, and even had hay in my mane. Oopsie!

Maureen

Seen a ghost

It was a windy day, and all the ponies in my group were on their toes. I trotted round with my rider but kept one eye on the outside of the arena, as I was sure something was going to jump out. Sure enough, a white thing bounced over the fence towards me. I instantly jumped out of the way, terrified that it was a ghost coming to get me! All the other ponies got scared, too, as they saw me panic, and one of the riders even fell off! Turned out it was just a plastic bag that had blown in. Silly me!

Calypso

World breeds
MARWARI

Learn more about this incredibly rare and hardy horse

Marwari horses hail from India and are a truly unique breed. They're famous for their beautiful, curved ears and graceful movement. Agile, intelligent and with tremendous stamina, Marwaris were originally bred as war horses, but are now growing in popularity as talented all-rounders.

Delving into history

Marwari horses were first bred in the 12th century by the Rathores, who ruled the Marwar region in western India. They bred tough, strong horses who went on to be favoured by the Indian cavalry. Marwaris were an ideal mount for the soldiers. As well as being brave and highly intelligent, they could cover long distances at speed, and were able to cope with intense heat and challenging conditions.

Being so majestic in looks and character, it's no surprise that Marwaris were also a firm favourite with the rulers of India. But, sadly, through no fault of their own, the breed began to decline in numbers during the 1930s. The horses that survived became working animals – a far cry from their regal heritage.

Luckily, the Marwari's fortunes were revived at the turn of this century, when efforts were made to save and promote the breed. A stud book has been started, which will help preserve this noble horse long into the future.

DID YOU KNOW?

As restrictions are in place on Marwaris being exported, the only place you'll see them is in their homeland of India.

FACT FILE

Height: 15hh to 16hh
Colour: Any colour is accepted, but grey horses are the most valuable.
Known for: Their curved ears, ambling gait and natural hardiness, loyalty and bravery.

Place of origin: The Marwar (or Jodhpur) region of India

Adapt and thrive

Marwari horses are perfectly designed to live in a hot, dry country. Their fine, silky coat helps keep them cool in the intense heat of summer, and long, elegant eyelashes protect their eyes in sandstorms. Those uniquely shaped ears, which touch at the tip, are not just beautiful to look at – they can rotate 180° to help prevent sand getting into them.

The Marwari's long, strong limbs are built for endurance, and the horses have a special gait, too, to give their riders a smoother journey. The rehwal or revaal is a four-beat gait that's said to be comfier than a trot.

The physical attributes of these amazing horses have helped them survive wars, droughts and tough conditions, and as the centuries have passed they've successfully adapted to cope with different lifestyles and challenges.

Family fortunes

It was once believed that Marwaris were descended from Arabian horses crossed with native ponies from India. Legend has it that seven shipwrecked Arabians are the founders of the Marwari breed. However, a recent study's revealed that this could be a myth. DNA research brought to light that Marwaris are more closely related to Turkoman, Akhal-Teke and Caspian horses. More studies are being carried out, so watch this space!

Born to dance

Marwaris are used for a whole range of activities, including endurance, showing and horse-back safaris, and some have ceremonial and religious roles, too. They're no longer used in the military, but are still popular in the Jodhpur and Jaipur regions of India.

They often take to the dressage arena like a duck to water, thanks to their natural love for performance. They're also used for polo, where they play against Thoroughbreds.

A relative of the Marwari, known as the Natchni, was believed to be 'born to dance'. They were dressed in jewels and bells and trained to perform spectacular routines at ceremonies, including weddings. While Natchni horses are now extinct, their dancing skills are still sought after in Marwari horses.

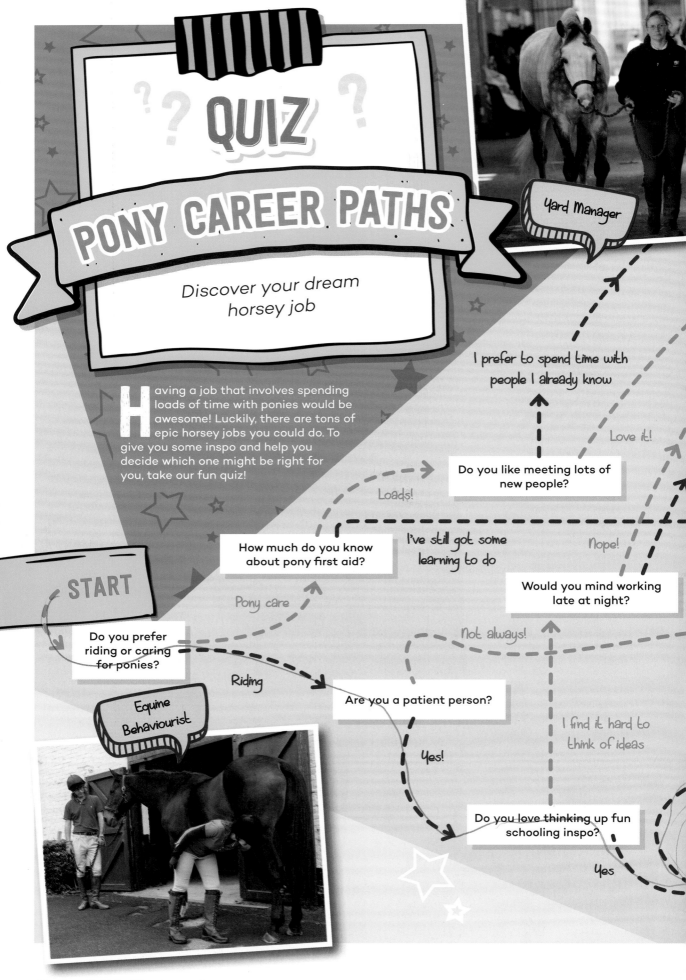

QUIZ

PONY CAREER PATHS

Discover your dream horsey job

Having a job that involves spending loads of time with ponies would be awesome! Luckily, there are tons of epic horsey jobs you could do. To give you some inspo and help you decide which one might be right for you, take our fun quiz!

Yard Manager

I prefer to spend time with people I already know

Love it!

Do you like meeting lots of new people?

Loads!

I've still got some learning to do

Nope!

How much do you know about pony first aid?

Would you mind working late at night?

Pony care

Not always!

START

Do you prefer riding or caring for ponies?

Riding

Equine Behaviourist

Are you a patient person?

I find it hard to think of ideas

Yes!

Do you love thinking up fun schooling inspo?

Yes

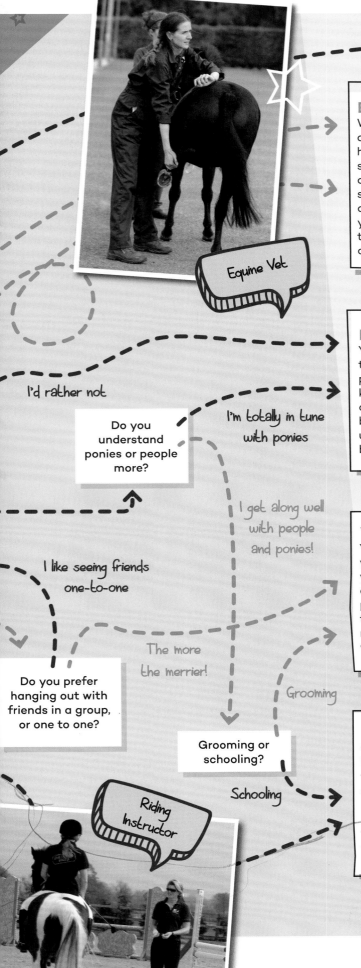

Equine Vet

EQUINE VET

What better job than helping ponies who are sick or injured feel better? You're patient, hardworking, and definitely not squeamish, so being an equine vet could be your perfect career path. Why not give yourself a head start by learning all you can about pony ailments and injuries? Your knowledge will help you care for your own fave pony and it's sure to come in handy if someone needs your help one day, too.

I'd rather not

Do you understand ponies or people more?

I'm totally in tune with ponies

EQUINE BEHAVIOURIST

You want every pony and rider to have fun together, so solving pony probs would be the perfect job for you! Equine behaviourists know all about how ponies think, and why they act like they do! It's a super-rewarding job because you'll help owners and their ponies understand each other better, so they can become besties for life!

I get along well with people and ponies!

I like seeing friends one-to-one

The more the merrier!

Grooming

YARD MANAGER

You love ponies and are super-organised, so you'd be brilliant at running a yard! Like you, yard managers are not afraid to get a little dirty mucking out stables and they can groom ponies to perfection! They know loads about them, too, so to help you prepare for this job, never miss an opportunity to learn as much as you can about riding and pony care!

Do you prefer hanging out with friends in a group, or one to one?

Grooming or schooling?

Schooling

Riding Instructor

RIDING INSTRUCTOR

Coming up with fun schooling exercises to try is your fave thing, which means you'd make a fab riding instructor one day! As well as being super-creative, you enjoy encouraging other riders to be the best they can, and find it really rewarding when you see them improve. Don't forget, it'll help if you're super-good at riding yourself, so practice, practice, practice!

GLOBAL CHAMPIONS TOUR

All about this awesome showjumping series

Do you love showjumping and want to watch the world's best riders and horses competing at the very top of their sport? Well, book your place on the 2021 Longines Global Champions Tour (LGCT)!

FAST FACTS

Where: All over the world, including London!
When: March-November
Why go: See the stars of showjumping in action

A grand tour

The Longines Global Champions Tour (LGCT) is a series of high-profile showjumping shows that take place all around the world. The biggest stars in the sport jump to win classes offering tempting prize money at each event, but the aim is also to collect points through the season. These points are awarded for each show's Grand Prix class and, at the end of the season, they're tallied up to find out who's the tour champion. Great Britain's Ben Maher has won this title twice — legendary!

DID YOU KNOW?

Half of the riders' best scores of the series count towards the overall Championship.

DID YOU KNOW?

Other riders also get a chance to compete at LGCT shows in two-star classes.

The wow factor

Unlike any event you'll have been to before, LGCT shows really do have the wow factor. Not only do they take place in glamorous locations, you may even spot some world-famous celebs in the audience. You'll feel a real buzz of excitement in the air, too.

Ride the world

The LGCT circuit travels across continents, with shows in some of the world's most famous cities, including Paris, Rome, Monaco, Madrid, Berlin, Mexico City, Shanghai, New York and Miami.

There's even a show in London, which is held at the Royal Hospital Chelsea, the home of British army veterans. Almost all of the LGCT venues are outdoors, so spectators can enjoy jaw-dropping backdrops to the showjumping action!

An exciting final is held in New York, at the end of the season, which is where the overall season champion is crowned.

Spectacular team fun

A unique team competition, The Global Champions League (GCL), has been created to add the fun factor to the tour! Top riders and talented U25 riders from different countries join together in teams with fun names such as the London Knights, Monaco Aces, Madrid in Motion and Shanghai Swans.

There are 16 teams in the league who compete through the season to try to top the leaderboard.

GC Prague Playoffs

Once the final has taken place, the LGCT and GCL action doesn't stop there! An exciting knock-out event has been created where riders battle all season to gain a golden ticket and qualify for the LGCT Super Grand Prix in a showdown with the best of the best. The winner of this will be crowned the ultimate Champion of Champions.

The GCL teams also compete in the prestigious GCL Super Cup in knock-out stages to decide the ultimate winners.

ALL THE INFO

For 2021 dates, and how you can watch from home, visit gcglobalchampions.com

HORSESCOPES

Find out what 2021 has in store for you and your fave pony...

ARIES
21 MAR – 20 APR

Your competitive edge will come out this year. You're sure to achieve loads with your fave pony, but be careful not to put too much pressure on him or yourself, as it's all meant to be fun!

TAURUS
21 APR – 21 MAY

This year's the perfect time to get to know your pony inside out! Make sure you spend lots of quality time together to keep your bond strong, by giving him a pamper sesh or teaching him tricks!

GEMINI
22 MAY – 22 JUN

Try new things with your fave pony this year, as you may discover something you really love! Why not have a go at a different discipline? It'll be super-fun for both him and you!

CANCER
23 JUN – 23 JUL

This year, you may be having thoughts that you aren't as good as someone else. Instead, try to focus on your own riding journey and keep persevering with lessons and training. You'll soon become an amazing rider!

LEO
24 JUL – 23 AUG

There's sure to be times when your fave pony might test your patience! Try and stay calm if things don't go to plan, and stick with your lessons, as you'll always manage to work it out in the end!

VIRGO
24 AUG – 23 SEP

There are lots of things you want to achieve with your fave pony, and you might be struggling to decide which one to do first! Think about which one you'd enjoy the most and focus on that!

LIBRA
24 SEP – 23 OCT

This year's all about learning for you. Take this as a sign to find out all you can about pony care and riding, so you become a pony whizz! Why not work towards a Pony Club efficiency test or badge?

SCORPIO
24 OCT – 22 NOV

You'll work well as part of a team this year. You'd enjoy competing on a Pony Club or Riding Club team with your pals, or joining in some group lessons. You're sure to meet a new friend or two if you do!

SAGITTARIUS
23 NOV – 22 DEC

You might have some fun riding a different pony than you're used to. It's good to get to know lots of types of ponies, as this will make you an even better rider!

AQUARIUS
19 JAN – 19 FEB

You're going to meet a special person this year who'll help you learn loads about ponies. There'll be some fun and exciting riding opportunities ahead, too, so make the most of them!

CAPRICORN
23 DEC – 19 JAN

Do you have some horsey goals you want to ace? This year will be lucky for you, so spend time planning how you're going to achieve them. You're sure to do well!

PISCES
20 FEB – 20 MAR

You may have a friend who needs your help with their pony. They might be lacking in confidence or feeling lonely and looking for someone to ride with. Make sure they know you're there to offer them a helping hand!

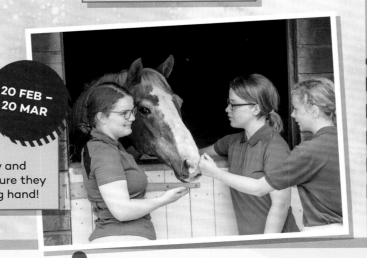

PONY MAG

MORE RIDING, MORE PONY CARE, MORE FUN!

Be a better rider with our fantastic training features and online videos

Learn everything you need to know about pony care

Keep up to date with the latest rider gossip and behind-the-scenes horsey action

See yourself in PONY

WIN awesome prizes in every issue of the magazine and online

PLUS cute posters, fun quizzes, cringeworthy horsey fess-ups, real-life dramas and loads more!

Join the PONY community at ponymag.com and on...

  facebook.com/ponymag @ponymaguk

ON SALE EVERY 4 WEEKS AT ALL GOOD NEWSAGENTS AND SUPERMARKETS

CUTE AS A BUTTON

Eight signs you have the cutest pony ever!

Of course every pony's super-adorable in their own way, but these tell-tale signs will let you know your fave pony has something really special about him. Do you recognise any of these cuteness clues?

1 Everyone wants him

If he's a riding school pony, everyone wants to ride him. If he's yours, all your friends wish they owned him. When your fave pony's popular with everyone he meets, then he's definitely super-cute – and not just to you!

2 He loves cuddles

Being cute isn't just about looks! A pony with a kind, gentle personality will make the best friend you could ask for and, if they're affectionate, too, they'll always put a smile on your face!

3 He has puppy dog eyes

Ponies have the largest eyes out of all land mammals, which helps make them look so cute to us! But if your pony's eyes are extra big and shiny, then he's bound to look even sweeter!

4 Judges love him

When you take your fave pony to a show he always gets a nice comment from the judge. In dressage you often get "lovely pony" on your score sheet, and out showing you always come home with a rosette!

5 He photographs well

Ponies often know how cute they are, and will pose perfectly when you point the camera at them! It means you can capture his adorableness and pop the picture up on your bedroom wall, or have it as your phone background.

6 You have a great bond

If you're riding or practising groundwork, your pony needs little encouragement to follow your instructions. He looks to you as his leader and, when people see how much you love each other, it's sure to melt their hearts!

7 He can do tricks

There's nothing more adorable than a pony who can perform cute tricks! Is yours clever enough to learn them? Having a special party trick like bowing on command or tapping a target with his nose will definitely win people over!

8 Even non-horsey people admire him

Do passers-by often stop to tell you how lovely your fave pony is while you're on a hack? Or maybe your non-horsey friends like and comment if you post an adorable pic of him on your Insta? Either way, if he gets compliments from people who aren't usually into horses, then he's definitely stunning to all!

PRZEWALSKI'S HORSE

Learn about the wild horses of Mongolia

Meet the Przewalski's Horse! They're really special because they're the only breed of horse that's truly wild. They look adorable with their spiky manes and cream-coloured muzzles, but they're super-tough, too! Learn all about what makes them so awesome!

Spike up

These horses have lots of unique characteristics that make them easy to identify! They're small and stocky, with a creamy coloured coat that fades in colour around their belly, and a black, spiky mane with no forelock. You'll see they have a black dorsal stripe that runs along their back, too, and a cream muzzle with black legs. They're closely related to the zebra and wild ass, and you can definitely see a resemblance!

Born to be wild

The Przewalski's Horse is thought to be the only wild horse that remains in the world. This is because their ancestors were never domesticated. All other wild horses are descended from ones who escaped captivity and became feral. However, the Przewalski's Horse was thought to have been extinct for many years, with their last sighting in 1969. However, by 1999 enough of the horses had been bred in captivity that they could be reintroduced to the wild.

DID YOU KNOW?

The largest number of wild Przewalski's Horses live at Hustai National Park in Mongolia.

FACT FILE

Height: 12hh to 14hh
Colour: Brindle – one of the rarest coat colours
Known for: Being the only truly wild horse left on earth

Place of origin: Mongolia

Not so chilly

Przewalski's Horses have to be able to cope with very cold, harsh environments, as the desert-like areas where they live can get extremely cold and windy! To help keep themselves warm, they grow long, super-thick coats in winter with long fluffy beards and extra neck hair. They tend to stand with their quarters to the wind, with their bushy tails in between their legs, to help protect themselves from dust.

Still in danger

The Przewalski's Horse is still classed as endangered, due to a loss of habitat, interbreeding and natural dangers such as harsh winters and predators. Thankfully, though, conservation schemes are helping the population slowly build in numbers again, as more horses are being bred in captivity and released into the wild every year.

Stay together

Like most feral horses, Przewalski's Horses tend to live in small groups called harems. They consist of around 5–15 horses, including one stallion, several mares and their foals. Sometimes, though, if a stallion can't find a harem, he'll form a group with other stallions, known as a bachelor group.

DID YOU KNOW?

There are only around 1,900 Przewalski's Horses in the World today.

T TRY THIS AT HOME!*

These adrenalin fuelled equestrian sports are sure to get your heart racing

If you thought jumping was daring, take a look at these extreme horsey sports. They test more than just your riding skills and are definitely not for the faint-hearted!

HORSEBACK ARCHERY

What? You'll need great balance, incredible hand-to-eye co-ordination and the perfect aim to ace horseback archery. It's essentially like normal archery, but you're aiming at the targets while on a cantering horse!

Where? There are clubs around the country that'll teach you the skills you need.

Find out more horsebackcombat.co.uk or bhaa.org.uk

TEAM CHASING

What? Taking cross-country to the next level, a team of riders follow each other round a formidable two-mile-long course of up to 25 fences, which could include huge hedges, daring drops and cavernous ditches! The aim's to be clear and fast.

Where? Team chases are held around the UK, and there's a spring season running from March to April and an autumn season with events from September to November.

Find out more teamchasing.co.uk

VAULTING

What? Vaulting's gymnastics on horseback. You can compete as an individual, in a pair or as part of a team, and the aim's to score high marks for the movements you're performing. Having the right horse is really important, as he'll need to canter in a steady, even rhythm for the whole of your routine.

Where? There are vaulting clubs all around the UK.

Find out more britishvaulting.org

DID YOU KNOW?

Vaulting's the only horse sport where a riding helmet isn't worn. This is because it would interfere with the movement and balance of the vaulter.

SNOW POLO

What? Polo requires speed, precision and awesome trust in your pony, which is a challenge in itself. But professional riders really take things to extremes when they play the game on snow and ice!

Where? There's a famous snow polo tournament every year, which takes place on a frozen lake in St Moritz, Switzerland.

Find out more snowpolo-stmoritz.com

HORSEBOARDING

What? Imagine balancing on a skateboard while being towed along by a galloping horse! Well, that's what horseboarding's all about! There are even competitions to take part in, where you'll need to negotiate a course of obstacles in the quickest time.

Where? Look out for horseboarding being demonstrated in the main arena at country fairs and county shows.

Find out more horseboardinguk.org

EXTREME DRIVING

What? Teams of four horses are driven at speed around a course of obstacles that has lots of twisty and tight turns. Drivers need to be super-accurate as well as fast, because if they dislodge a ball they'll get time penalties.

Where? It's a firm favourite with spectators at Windsor and Olympia Horse Shows.

Find out more olympiahorseshow.com or rwhs.co.uk

* HONESTLY, DON'T! None of these activities should be attempted without proper training and equipment!

TO THE RESCUE

FIRST AID
EMERGENCY MANUAL

Sasha and Aidan never thought they'd turn into heroes on their hack

Aidan and I were sat in a classroom at our Pony Club first aid rally. There were 10 of us in the group, and we'd been watching our instructor show us how to put someone into the recovery position. "What's the point in learning this stuff anyway? It's not like we'll ever use it," Aidan whispered in my ear. "Shh, I'm trying to listen," I replied.

Even though I found what we were learning quite interesting, I knew Aidan would much rather be jumping over fences on his pony, Quest. He sighed as the instructor handed us all a pouch each. I had a quick peak inside and found it was full of first aid stuff like plasters, wipes and even a bandage.

We all stood up from our chairs as our instructor said the session was over for the day. "Anyway," I said to Aidan, as we walked out of the classroom. "How do you know this stuff won't come in handy one day? What if one of us falls off our pony?" He rolled his eyes at me. "I'm sure we'll be fine, Sasha," he replied. "None of us have fallen off in ages."

Something in the woods

The following afternoon, Aidan and I were tacking up our ponies ready to go for a hack. I couldn't wait to ride my pony, Butterbean, but Aidan was a bit of a daredevil, and I was slightly worried he'd want to canter everywhere.

Knowing he'd make fun of me if he saw, I snuck my saddlebag on, and popped my mini first aid kit from the rally inside, without him noticing.

"Are you going to the next first aid rally?" I asked him as he walked over with his riding stuff on. Aidan shook his head before mounting up. "No, I was so bored yesterday. I think that badge is overrated." I tutted at him before climbing onto Butterbean.

It was a lovely sunny day and we were having an awesome time on our ponies. We'd enjoyed a canter along a track and were both buzzing. "See? Isn't this so much better than a boring rally?" Aidan laughed, giving Quest a scratch on the neck.

We chatted as we rode and turned onto a bridleway that led through some woods. As we ventured between the trees, we heard a strange noise. The ponies stopped and pricked their ears. It sounded like someone crying. "Did you hear that?" I asked Aidan.

"Yeah, I did," he said.

> ❝ It wasn't long before we heard sirens, and two paramedics came running ❞

Call to action

"Hello? Is someone there?" I called out. To our surprise, a weak voice replied. "Hello? Yes, I'm down here, and I need some help!" Aidan and I walked the ponies towards the voice, scanning the undergrowth. "There!" Aidan said, pointing at the bushes. We halted, and quickly jumped off. "Hello?" I called again, handing Butterbean's reins to Aidan.

A girl a little older than us was laying on the ground. She was wearing a riding hat, looked very pale and had a cut on her face.

"Oh my gosh, are you OK?" I gasped.

"I've really hurt my arm," she said, wincing in pain. "Where did your pony go?" Aidan asked, looking around to see if he was nearby. "I don't know," she replied. "He spooked at a deer and galloped back the way we came. Did you see him?"

"No, we didn't, I'm really sorry," replied Aidan.

"We need to make sure you're OK, though, before we look for him." I took charge. "Aidan, can you phone for help?" I went back over to Butterbean and took the mini first aid kit out of my saddlebag. I saw Aidan look but, instead of laughing, he seemed quite scared.

"Who should I call?" he asked, meekly. "I think we should call for an ambulance, but I'm not sure where we are," I replied.

"This bridleway comes out onto the road we drive along to get to my grandparents' house. I think I can direct them," he said bravely, while dialling 999.

I left Aidan with the ponies and went over to the girl with my first aid kit. She tried to take her hat off, but I shook my head quickly, remembering what we'd been taught at the first aid rally. "Keep your hat on in case you banged your head when you fell," I said, before taking an antiseptic wipe and a pair of gloves out of my first aid kit, and gently cleaning the cut on her face. She winced a bit, but was super-brave. "I'm Sasha and that's Aidan, by the way. What's your name?" I asked, trying to distract her from the stinging.

"Wendy," she said. "I'm so glad you're both here, thank you for helping me."

I checked there wasn't any dirt in the cut one more time. "All done! It's not too deep so I don't think it needs a plaster or anything. They told us yesterday that grazes are best left in the fresh air, right Aidan?"

I looked over at him and he nodded slowly, clearly feeling a little sheepish for making fun of me earlier.

"The ambulance is on its way," he said, leading the ponies over to us. I was really impressed with how great he'd been at calling the ambulance – I would have been sooo nervous!

Pony hunting!

It wasn't long before we heard sirens, and two paramedics came running. One of them knelt down beside Wendy, and started asking her questions about what had happened. The other told us we'd done the right thing by calling them.

"It's a good job you two were here," she added." We'll make sure this young lady's taken care of. Are you going to be okay getting home?"

We said we would be, and used a nearby tree stump as a makeshift mounting block.

"Hey, do you think we should try to find Wendy's pony?" Aidan said, as we started walking back along the path.

"That's a great idea!" I replied. We followed the bridleway, scanning the ground for clues. "Look, Sasha! Are those hoofprints? He must've gone that way!" Aidan started trotting in the direction of the prints and Butterbean and I followed.

As we emerged from the trees, we found ourselves in an open field. We narrowed our eyes as we caught sight of an orange blob in the middle of the grass. "That's him!" whispered Aidan.

We tentatively rode up to the chestnut pony, and he pricked his ears when he saw us. Aidan quickly dismounted, handing me Quest's reins, and carefully approached the pony, offering him a treat. The pony gratefully accepted it, and Aidan was able to take hold of his bridle. He ran up the stirrups, and started leading him and Quest back towards the woods, while I paved the way on Butterbean. Wendy would be so pleased!

Reunited

"Reggie!" Wendy shouted, as we approached the ambulance crew again. The paramedic asked her to sit still, but let Aidan bring Reggie over to her. She stroked his face and kissed his nose, obviously over the moon to have him back.

"Thank you sooo much for finding him! Is he OK?" she asked, tears welling up in her eyes.

"He was munching some grass when we found him. He did have his reins in knots, but I can't see any injuries," Aidan said.

Wendy's mum had just arrived after the paramedics called her, and we handed Reggie to her.

"They want to take her to the hospital for X-rays to see if anything's broken," she told us. "We can't thank you enough for acting so quickly. I was worried sick when Wendy wasn't back when she said she would be. But you best be off now, as it'll be getting dark soon," she continued. Aidan hopped back onto Quest and we headed home.

"What a day!" I sighed, suddenly feeling exhausted.

"I can't believe we really used that first aid stuff we learnt," Aidan said, suddenly looking sheepish. "Sorry I made fun of you for listening at the rally, Sasha. I'm so glad Wendy's okay. And…" he looked down. "I think I will come to the next one with you."

I smiled at him. "Glad to hear it! You were amazing on the phone, and catching Reggie like that was so brave!" Aidan laughed off my compliment.

"Well, I think we definitely deserve our first aid badge after all that!"

THE ANSWERS

Page 44 — GET SET AND VET QUIZ

1 B, **2** C, **3** B, C, E **4** A, **5** A, **6** C, **7** B, **8** A, **9** B, **10** A,

Page 70 — CARE PACKAGE QUIZ

1 B, **2** A, **3** C, **4** A, **5** B, **6** A, **7** C, **8** A, **9** B, **10** A

Page 52 — MEGA PONY PUZZLES

▶ **Tack teaser wordsearch**

```
U L B A N D A G E S S D B K J G
S H U E L A G N I T R A M N O R
H T G N G F O H A O S O T I A A
G X O I G S C B E O E E E L U S
R U R O E E L R P B E Z N S T R
L T R B B E C A V H R H N I I E
H E A R W L R A S C E Y O R R I
B N A R E T E E V A S X B R U N
D R A D S L S V D E S F R U P S
Z P I K R I O C A R S D A P I S
S B C D C O O O B R F S E I R S
U E P R L L P I C E T M O E I V
N A E U L E T E S V N W N N R H
D X C A G U R T U O N R U T O G
E B R U S H I N G B O O T S N I
E G A D N A B L I A T G I Q S H
```

▶ On the fence

1 Water Tray

2 Wall

3 Planks

4 Oxer

5 Cross-pole

▶ Spot the difference

MAKE TEMPLATE ♥

Page 12

MAKE A PONY PRINT CANVAS

Trace the templates, draw them on to card, then cut them out.

THE MISADVENTURES OF CHARLIE!